HOW A CAREER IN REAL ESTATE?

CARLA CROSS

**Real Estate
Education Company**
a division of Dearborn Financial Publishing, Inc.

While a great deal of care has been taken to provide accurate and current information, the ideas, suggestions, general principles and conclusions presented in this text are subject to local, state and federal laws and regulations, court cases and any revisions of same. The reader is thus urged to consult legal counsel regarding any points of law—this publication should not be used as a substitute for competent legal advice.

Publisher: Kathleen A. Welton
Acquisitions Editor: Patrick J. Hogan
Associate Editor: Karen A. Christensen
Senior Project Editor: Jack L. Kiburz
Interior Design: Lucy Jenkins
Cover Design: Michael S. Finkelman, Shot in the Dark Design

Published by Real Estate Education Company
a division of Dearborn Financial Publishing, Inc.

Printed in the United States of America.

93 94 95 10 9 8 7 6 5 4 3 2 1

Library of Congress Cataloging-in-Publication Data

Cross, Carla
   How about a career in real estate? / by Carla Cross.
    p. cm.
   Includes bibliographical references.
   ISBN 0-7931-0745-8
   1. Real estate business—Vocational guidance. I. Title.
HD1375.C68 1993   93-14477
333.33′023′73—dc20   CIP

Contents

Preface

What is success to you? Is it having the money to fulfill your dreams? Security for your family? The ability to help others—to make a positive change in their lives? A career in real estate can give you not only security but also financial rewards and prestige. In addition, you will enjoy emotional satisfaction as you help customers and clients enjoy a better life. For most Americans, the equity in their homes is the *only* substantial "savings account" they have to finance retirement. Real estate professionals help buyers and sellers with the personal and often difficult decisions concerning this unique investment.

But is a career in real estate *for you?* After all, there are other ways to obtain your version of success. I wrote this book to help you thoroughly investigate real estate as a career and decide if it is the right choice for you.

Many new agents enter real estate with a short-term vision, giving rise to the high turnover so common to our industry—the revolving door. It doesn't have to be that way. Too many agents take an unrealistic approach, obtaining a license with the plan to give real estate a try for a few months to see if they can make some sales.

By understanding the nature of the business, you can take a long-term approach to your career. High-producing agents tell me that it took them two to three years to establish a career that produced the benefits they expected from the business.

The real estate industry is changing dramatically. Whereas in the past the more "bodies" the better, in the 1990s the trend is toward fewer, but more *committed* salespeople. I call these people careerists because real estate sales is a serious career choice for them, and they expect real estate sales to give them an income equal to that of other professions they could enter. Willing to invest their personal and financial resources to be successful, the best agents look at real estate as an attractive opportunity to be in business for themselves. In this book, I will show how you can take advantage of these and other trends to build a dynamic real estate career.

Although I have tried to convey standard practices, real estate can be difficult to standardize; each city, or section of a city, has individual real estate practices. I could by no means explain all the variations of practices in this book; however, it can serve as a guide to open discussions. It should not be used to assert the correctness of a particular real estate practice.

I have seen all types of people enter the profession during 20 years of real estate experience as a top salesperson, trainer and broker-manager for a large independent company. Some did very well, others languished. Finally, tired of seeing new agents caught in the revolving door, I decided to help them.

I developed a training program for my company, Windermere Real Estate, and served as a mentor for new agents. In addition, my experience as an instructor of designated courses (GRI and CRB, see Appendix D) has given me the opportunity to visit and study top companies across the nation. By observing traits and behaviors of various salespeople, I began to see patterns of success and failure. As a manager, I put these discoveries to work by hiring winners and helping them develop six-figure careers quickly. This book will help you identify your winning characteristics and create your own success in real estate.

The nineties holds fantastic opportunity for dedicated real estate salespeople. Not only can careerists make large incomes, they also can set the standards of practice for an industry that has been working hard to promote professionalism. You have the opportunity to develop your individual talents and provide the level of service customers and clients expect in this decade. I want to extend my best wishes to you as you investigate this vibrant, exciting and challenging career.

Acknowledgments

This book could not be written without the contributions of the industry insiders who created and/or provided some of the statistical research:

- Steve Francis, Executive Officer of the National Association of Real Estate Licensing Law Officials, (NARELLO) provided much of the information about licensing requirements.
- Nancy Draper, of the Washington Department of Licensing, Real Estate Division, provided in-depth information concerning licensing statistics.
- The media department of the National Association of REALTORS® contributed research and recommended sources.
- John Tuccillo, Chief Economist for the National Association of REALTORS®, conducted research invaluable in guiding real estate professionals to make the right decisions.
- Richard W. Schmidt, Selection Services Marketing for Life Insurance Marketing and Research Association (LIMRA) provided insights into new real estate selection systems.

Through two decades of various real estate activities, I have learned from some of the best in the business—the agents, managers, owners, and trainers with whom I have been privileged to work. A special acknowledgment to the agents of both of my offices, who provided me with the most valuable information I pass along in this book. Through their examples of professionalism, they taught me how to spot winners. A special tribute, too, to the agents quoted here who contributed advice to help you make a good career decision.

Although specific to real estate, this book also reflects experiences with the people who have "writ big" in my life:

- My parents, Bob and Eleanora Garrison, who taught me that unconditional love and support create the self-confidence to succeed in a challenging endeavor such as real estate sales
- My sister, Laura Bruyneel, whose intelligent, innovative approach to seemingly insurmountable obstacles demonstrates that anything is possible if you just make a few creative runs at it—and laugh at your mistakes as you go
- The many mentors in my life, who sometimes saw in me abilities that I didn't know I possessed

To all of them—thank you.

1 Welcome to the World of Real Estate Sales

"As a new agent, I have learned that this job creates high demands. You have to love it. I do. I have a passion for real estate!"

—Tim Smallwood, top producer his first year, formerly trainer/salesperson in another sales career

In This Chapter . . . .

- The exciting world of real estate sales
- *Agent, broker, agency* defined
- How real estate salespeople are paid
- Commissions between companies
- Typical commission structures
- Business and legal affiliations
- The activities of a real estate agent
- Differences between real estate sales and other sales positions

The Excitement and Challenge of Real Estate Sales

In a recent survey by a major real estate company, agents were asked why they went into real estate. They answered:

- To be their own bosses
- For the freedom

- Because they like people
- To be different
- To meet new challenges

For many people, real estate sales offers a career of almost unlimited income potential and challenge. In fact, real estate is one of the last frontiers of business opportunity in the United States. One can get into real estate sales easily, with few educational requirements and little cash outlay.

If it's such a wonderful career, why do many agents go into—and out of—the business each year? It has been estimated that one-fourth to one-third of all the real estate agents actively selling real estate have less than one year's experience in the business. And, in a recent study by the National Association of REALTORS® (NAR), the average time in the business was only four years. Most agents fail because they do not know enough to make an informed career decision. Some underestimate the number of hours per week required to build the business. Some misunderstand that *independence* includes all the considerations and responsibilities of starting a small business—budgeting, time management, start-up costs and business planning. Some fail because they assume business will fall in their laps, so they sit and wait until their money runs out. The goal of this book is to give you information about real estate as a career:

- What selling real estate is—the day-to-day job
- The qualities and traits required to succeed in real estate
- The activities that ensure success in real estate sales
- The costs associated with the job
- The steps to find and associate with an office

Armed with this information, you can make a good decision about real estate sales as a career for you. And, if you decide to enter the field, you'll have all the tools to choose the company, office, manager and associates that are right for you.

Before launching into a description of real estate sales, you should understand the basic language of the world of real estate.

What Is a Real Estate Agent?

The language of real estate can be confusing. The terms *agent* and *broker* are used interchangeably, although they refer to two different real estate licenses. Agents are licensed as real estate salespersons, allowing them to legally collect commissions on the sale of real estate. However, an agent can't collect these commissions directly. Any commissions paid to the agent must be paid through the person with whom the agent is licensed. This person is called a *designated broker* and is licensed with a state-licensed real estate company. Here is the path up the chain of command:

1. State-licensed real estate salesperson
2. Supervision by a licensed real estate broker (designated broker)
3. Broker affiliation with a state-licensed real estate company

Later, this chapter will go further into these relationships. Generally, real estate agents are not employed by a real estate company. Instead, agents sign an *independent contractor* agreement that states an individual is contracting with a real estate company for services provided. In this arrangement, the real estate agent pays his own taxes, including Social Security tax, and is responsible for his own health insurance, personal injury insurance and retirement planning.

More about the Broker

The broker's license is earned by a person who

- has been licensed in real estate for one to three years, depending on the state's requirements where he or she is licensed;
- has completed a specific course curriculum, as set by each state (from 15 to 225 hours); and
- passes an exam.

Check with your state regulatory agency for your specific standards. Appendix B lists contact people for your jurisdiction.

The term *broker* is used to describe several situations:

- *The designated broker*: A person who has been licensed by a state regulatory agency to "supervise and be responsible for" the salespeople licensed to that particular company. In order to be a designated broker, the person must hold a broker's license and be registered as the designated broker to the state regulatory agency. There is only one designated broker per company.

- The *manager of an office* (may be called a branch manager): A person in most states who must hold a broker's license, and is responsible for recruiting, selecting, training, retaining and terminating sales associates. Through these activities, he or she is responsible to the owner to *make a profit* for the office.
- The *associate brokers*: Agents who hold a broker's license but who may not manage salespeople. An associate broker earns broker's license because the public recognizes the license as a differentiator. In fact, the public sometimes calls *all* licensees brokers. In some states, one-tenth of all licensees are brokers. In a few states, the only license available is the broker's license. Check with your state regulatory agency for specifics in your state.

Agent Specialties

According to a National Association of REALTORS® survey, agents selling residential properties accounted for 71 percent of NAR members. The next largest group (8 percent) sold commercial and industrial properties. Property managers accounted for 6 percent, and others who sold no properties but were affiliated with NAR accounted for another 10 percent. Because most agents sell residential properties, the examples in this book are residential. However, the principles of business development, business planning and budgeting, are the same for all sales specialties.

Agency Relationships

All real estate licensees are governed by the *law of agency*. This law spells out where a licensee's fiduciary duty lies and how he or she is to be responsible to his or her principals. *Principals* can be sellers, buyers and real estate agencies. Historically, residential agents made contractual agreements only with sellers and, through those agreements, were responsible to act in the sellers' best interest. Recently, though, licensees have begun making contractual relationships with buyers. This new agency relationship, termed *buyer agency,* has caused much confusion and debate among real estate licensees and consumers. There are many conflicting relational and contractual implications to these agency questions. State regulatory agencies, REALTOR® associations and real estate companies are struggling to redefine contractual relationships with buyers and sellers. This decade will see continuing debate as licensees struggle to conform to the laws, to fulfill their legal responsibilities and to clarify these very complex issues.

Besides referring to the law, the word *agency* also is commonly used as another name for a real estate company. All agencies, or companies, are licensed by the state in which they are located and are subject to the state's laws, rules and regulations regarding real estate practice (the laws of agency). Each company must employ a designated broker, who is responsible for supervising all licensees licensed with that agency. The designated broker is often the owner, but sometimes is someone other than the owner—for example, an agent with a broker's license who agrees to carry this responsibility. Generally, a branch manager is not the designated broker.

How Real Estate Salespeople Are Paid

Almost all real estate salespeople are paid through the commissions they earn. There is no salary, and new agents generally cannot draw salary against future commissions. Agents earn a commission (paid through their company) when they sell a home or when a home they have listed is sold by them or by another agent. *Listing* a home for sale means that the agent signs some type of agreement to sell with a homeowner. The agent, referred to as a *listing agent*, markets the property to other agents and to the public. In the most common type of listing agreement, the seller in return promises to pay a commission to the listing agency when a buyer purchases the property. If the listing company also sells the property, the company receives the whole commission and distributes part of it to the agent or agents who listed and sold the property. If another company sells the property, part of the commission is paid to the *selling agency*. (See Figure 1.1.)

Figure 1.1   How Commissions Are Shared

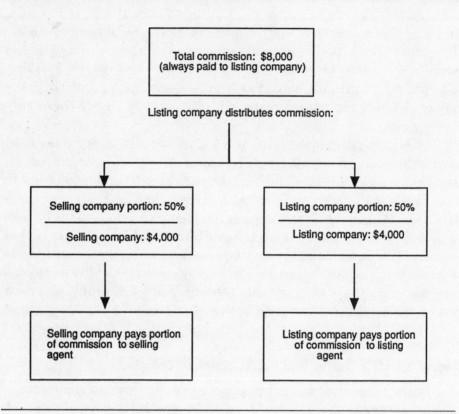

When Are Commissions Paid?   Agents are paid only when buyers finalize the sale on a property (termed *closing*). This means that all paperwork regarding the transaction has been completed, and the monetary proceeds are available to the seller. Closing takes about two months from the date the offer to purchase is signed and accepted by the seller. Agents are *paid only for closings of properties listed, not for listing them*. In fact, not all properties listed actually sell. In one study, of all the homes listed in an area, less than half the properties listed during a half-year period actually sold!

How Much Is a Sale Worth?   How much does the agent earn when he or she lists or sells a home? Let's walk through how commissions are computed and divided. Commissions are generally based on the sale price of the property. Less commonly used methods to collect sales fees are as follows:

- A flat fee paid by the seller (sometimes charged wholly or partially whether or not the home is sold)
- A commission based on listed price or sales price and paid by the buyer

Each company sets its rate of commission, and fees vary depending on the services the company provides. For example, a company pays 6 percent commission. The total commission on closing of a $100,000 home (at 6 percent) is $6,000. This commission is divided between the companies involved in the transaction. Each company, in turn, pays the agent according to the contract agreement the agent signed with the company.

Commission Splits and Company Services

To receive a commission as a licensed real estate agent, agents must be affiliated with a licensed real estate company. All commissions due are paid to the company, and the company distributes the agent's portion to the agent. That portion varies from company to company. Here are four of the most common ways commissions are shared between company and agent:

1. *a sliding scale:* At the beginning of the year (either a calendar year or the agent's hiring anniversary), the agent splits the total commission dollars earned pretty evenly (like 50/50) between the agent and the company. As the year progresses and the agent is paid commissions, the agent reaches certain *paid commission plateaus*. These plateaus are computed by the amount of commissions generated by that agent and paid to the company. After the agent reaches a plateau, the agent is paid an increasingly greater percent of the total commission dollars.

   Example: As a new agent, you sell a home listed by another company. The total commission paid is $6,000. The listing company receives $3,000. According to your agreement with your company, you receive 50 percent of that commission, or

$1,500. In July, you receive notice that, from your listings sold and sales closed, $36,000 has been paid to you and your company. Because you were on a 50/50 split, half of the commissions paid to the company from your closings go to you—and half to your company. So, $18,000 in commissions has been paid to date to your company and $18,000 has been paid to you. Your plateau is $18,000. You have reached that plateau. On your next commission, you receive 70 percent of the total commission. Right after you receive notice of your increased commission split, your listed property is sold by another company. The total commission due your company is $4,000. So, you receive 70 percent of that commission, or $2,800. Your company receives $1,200.

Companies typically have two or three gradations in their commission plan, and these plateaus vary with companies. Some companies have many plans available to their agents.

2. *desk fee:* The total commission paid on a sale or listing is passed through the company to the agent. The company pays its expenses (and makes a profit) from a "desk fee" paid by the agent. Desk fees range from approximately $300 to about $2,000 per month. On the low end, this fee merely pays for desk space in an office. On the high end are offices that provide elaborate decor, mechanical support (the latest in computers, etc.), support staff and marketing materials. Paying a desk fee places the agent truly in business for himself or herself, planning, budgeting, and implementing his business plan independently. The agent has the benefit of the company "umbrella," which may include institutional (image) advertising and marketing pieces. Because all expenses are borne by the agent, few new agents opt for a desk fee office. And since going it alone takes time and expertise, it is estimated that desk fee agents actually retain about 65 percent of their gross dollars—a ratio comparable to traditional, or funded offices as in the first example.

3. *fee-based:* Some companies have a menu of services that are offered to sellers or buyers. Agents in these companies are paid a portion of the fees paid by the consumer. For example, rather than pay for the service a seller may choose to show his or her own

home. He or she pays fees to the listing company for listing with the multiple listing service and fees for various advertising services.

4. *salaried:* Although not common in the industry, a few companies are offering salaries, or base salaries plus commission. Look for variations of these payment plans in the nineties, as the complexities of representation create new opportunities for real estate specialists. (See Figure 1.2.)

There are many variations on these themes, and more to come in the nineties as companies struggle to make a profit while attracting good agents. According to the National Association of REALTORS® study of 1991, real estate companies increased their gross revenues for the three years from 1988 to 1991. However, operating expenses increased from 31 percent to 35 percent. Also, the portion of gross commissions paid to salespeople increased by 9 percent. So profits shrank!

Agency Service Reductions   Along with these commission plans come various services but there's no free lunch. In general, the more generous the commission to the agent, the fewer services are free to the agent. This relationship is represented in Figure 1.3.

As the agent captures more of the gross commission dollar, services that real estate companies can afford to provide to agents must shrink.

Professional Affiliations

The Multiple Listing Service (MLS)

Many times, your listing will be sold by another company or you will sell a home listed by another company. Access to homes listed by other companies and information about other companies' listed properties are furnished through membership in a *multiple listing service,* a cooperative group of real estate companies. These services were formed in communities to increase the exposure of listed properties to agents and to the public. Multiple listing services cooperate in

---

Figure 1.2   A Typical Graduated Commission Schedule

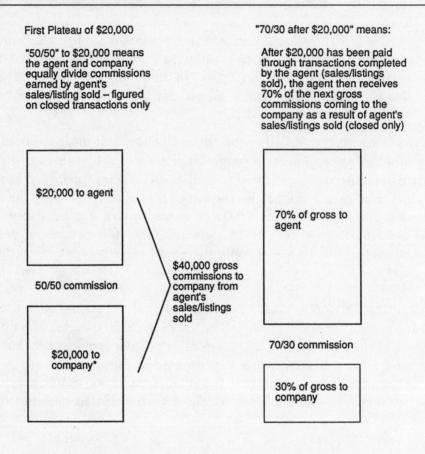

First Plateau of $20,000

"50/50" to $20,000 means the agent and company equally divide commissions earned by agent's sales/listing sold – figured on closed transactions only

"70/30 after $20,000" means:

After $20,000 has been paid through transactions completed by the agent (sales/listings sold), the agent then receives 70% of the next gross commissions coming to the company as a result of agent's sales/listings sold (closed only)

$20,000 to agent

50/50 commission

$20,000 to company*

$40,000 gross commissions to company from agent's sales/listings sold

70% of gross to agent

70/30 commission

30% of gross to company

* *Company* must be paid $20,000 to 'trigger' the next plateau

---

promoting each others' listings, disseminating information, settling disputes between members and providing ancillary services such as health insurance plans and credit union memberships. Most residential real estate companies today belong to a multiple listing service. Agent-members of these companies pay monthly fees to the MLS to receive information via computer and/or printed materials about current and past property listings. With membership, the agent has

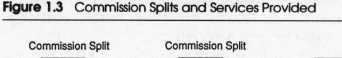

Figure 1.3   Commission Splits and Services Provided

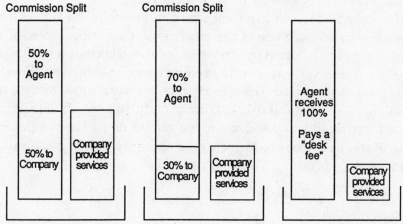

the right to sell properties listed through the service and to receive a portion of the commission, paid through his or her company.

The relationships formed by memberships in multiple listing services (or through certain kinds of representation) are governed by the laws of agency and by multiple listing rules. So, when a home is listed by a member of the multiple listing service, other members of the service automatically become *subagents,* representing the seller's interest through their relationships in their MLS. Agency disclosure issues have become complex partly because of these inherent agency relationships. The conflicts of interest that can occur in some selling situations causes fierce debate on this issue.

Realtor® Affiliation

The National Association of REALTORS® (NAR) is by far the largest professional organization of real estate licensees in the United States. With 750,000 members (out of a total of 1.2 million active licensees), NAR includes all specializations of real estate and provides member services, education, political information and lobbying for private property rights. It holds members to ethical standards of practice as spelled out in the REALTORS® Code of Ethics. Members, as well as the public, have the right to hold REALTOR® members to the Code via a hearing process executed by local Associations.

Active membership within local, state and national REALTOR® associations has provided some of the most rewarding experiences of my real estate career. Interest in education led me to become a local, state and national chairperson of various educational committees. Working for this good cause affords the opportunity to return something to this profession, raise its standards and make enduring, invaluable friendships. Of course, like any endeavor, you get out of it what you put into it. One of the best ways to launch your career is to join a committee at your local association. These include:

- Governmental Affairs
- Member Services
- Standards of Practice
- Education
- Special Events

You will immediately feel as though you are "in the business." You will learn so much so fast. You will be working with the "cream of the crop"—and you will establish a valuable referral base with other pros. NAR members work to raise the standards of professionalism throughout the real estate industry.

Continuing Education Opportunities One of NAR's greatest contributions to the profession has been its establishment of continuing education courses. For your career development, state and national REALTOR® organizations offer a series of courses that are listed in Appendix C. Most of the courses NAR sponsors lead to professional designations in real estate specialty areas. Besides raising the level of professionalism internally, NAR efforts have enabled the public to experience an increasingly higher level of customer service. And, since highly satisfied customers and clients return—and provide referrals—the National Association of REALTORS® continues to provide valuable benefits to both its consumer groups—the public and NAR members. An agent pays membership dues to belong to the local, state, and national associations. In some areas, NAR and multiple listing services are combined. Check your area for affiliations and costs.

NAREB Membership

National Association of Real Estate Brokers, Inc. (NAREB), the oldest and largest minority trade association in America, was founded in 1947. Members, called *Realtists*, are pledged to provide "democracy in housing." This organization consists of eight professional affiliates. Realtists work with the government and the private sector to provide housing for minorities.

Figure 1.4 shows how all these organizations—your company, REALTOR® organizations, multiple listing services and regulatory agencies interact.

What a Real Estate Agent Does

Now you understand the basic language. Let's get to the nuts and bolts of the business. There are literally dozens of activities that, as an agent, you can take part in during your business week, such as the following:

- Previewing your office's new listings on office tour
- Previewing properties listed by other agencies
- Completing paperwork on transactions
- Following up with customers/clients
- Following up with prospects
- Setting showing appointments
- Showing properties to buyers
- Attending office meetings
- Attending educational sessions
- Attending REALTOR® meetings/committee work
- Finding potential customers/clients
- Doing listing presentations
- Learning about title, escrow, closing procedures
- Organizing materials/your desk
- Answering calls at office on schedule assigned by office (commonly called floor time)

Figure 1.4   How Real Estate Organizations Relate

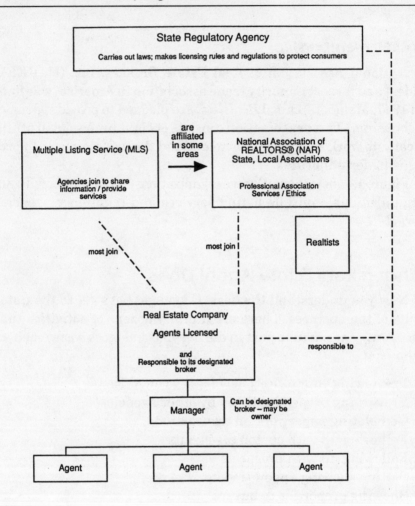

- Holding open houses for the public
- Holding open houses for the cooperating agents (brokers' opens)
- Preparing brochures for properties
- Promoting yourself (preparing brochures, cards, etc., to mail to identified markets/other promotions to increase name recognition)
- Following up on transactions to the end of the transaction (closings)

- Studying finance options
- Planning your days, weeks—long-term goals

As new agents quickly learn, the number of activities one can do seems endless.

Income-Generating Activities

There are certain critical activities agents *must* perform in order to get paid, such as prospecting to find buyers and sellers, listing salable properties and selling properties. Figure 1.5 shows the flow of business, from meeting people to earning a paycheck.

This stream of *income-generating activities,* only when consistently initiated and followed, leads to results—sales and listings sold—

Figure 1.5 Critical Activity Flow

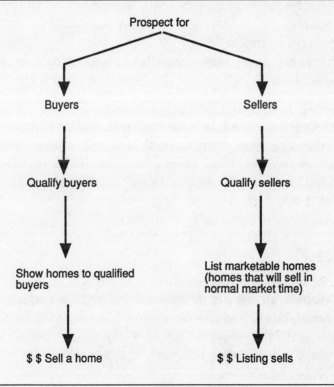

$$$. Agents who create careers fast do many business-producing, critical activities. They do only enough *support activities* (paperwork, etc.) to maintain their business production.

Differences Between Real Estate Sales and Other Sales Positions

Selling real estate is not like selling automobiles or pharmaceuticals. In fact, there are four major differences between real estate sales and other commissioned sales positions:

1. Real estate salespeople must *go out and find leads*—people who are prospective sellers and purchasers; few prospects are given to the agents by management.
2. Relatively little business is generated through walk-ins—people who come into the office and want to list or sell real estate (unlike automobile sales or retail sales).
3. Real estate salespeople cannot depend on media advertising (newspaper, TV, etc.) to generate enough calls to them to meet their income expectations.
4. Unlike some sales businesses (pharmaceuticals or radio time sales) real estate salespeople have no assigned territory.

In general, generating prospects is almost solely up to the real estate salesperson. That is why the field enjoys almost unlimited earning potential. And, ironically, that is one reason why so many people fail in real estate in their first year. Not understanding the nature of the business, they sit and wait for prospects instead of going out to find them.

Summary

This chapter is your introduction to the world of real estate sales. Because almost all agents are contracted with a company as independent contractors, real estate salespeople are really in business for themselves, with the responsibilities of paying quarterly taxes, social security tax and budgeting income and expenses (more about this in Chapter 5).

Contrary to popular belief, real estate salespeople are generally paid no salary, have no expense accounts and generally receive no draw against future commissions. They earn a paycheck from the commissions they are paid. Commission plans vary. Generally, the more generous the commission split to the agent, the fewer services are provided for free.

Real estate sales is different from other sales positions. Prospects generally do not come to the real estate salesperson as they do in other sales positions. Real estate salespeople must go out and find prospects. For those with business savvy, energy and enthusiasm, a career in real estate can be financially and emotionally rewarding because success in real estate depends largely on the personal efforts of the individual.

2 What It Takes To Succeed

"New agents are often advised to buy all sorts of tools and spend lots of money (car phones, tape recorders, sonic measuring devices, massive mail-outs, etc.), but the only message that needs to be stressed and restressed is to prospect a major portion of your day. Get the scripts and dialogues needed to cold call, door knock, work expireds and FSBOs. Do the work, and you'll become a great, consistently high producing agent."

—Rick Franz, top producer within two years, formerly in restaurant management

In This Chapter . . . .

- Your ideal job and real estate sales—a match?
- Qualities of successful salespeople
- How to determine if you have those qualities

. . . .

You and Real Estate—A Career Match?

Here's the scenario—a common one that frequently piques an individual's attention and turns his interest to real estate sales. You've just bought your new home. You enjoyed working with a real estate agent. Coincidentally disenchanted with your current position as a sales representative for a national company, you start thinking about real estate sales as a career alternative.

Like you, thousands of people each year consider real estate sales as a career change. Frequently, their outside-in view of real estate sales leads them to charge full force into the field—and find out later that what they thought they were getting wasn't what they got! So that you can avoid leaping before you look, here is a way to see if your ideal job is real estate sales. This chapter will show you the qualities that make real estate salespeople successful. Do-it-yourself inventories will help you search for those qualities within yourself and create a futuristic picture of yourself in real estate. That way, you can evaluate

- whether your ideal job and real estate sales are a match and
- whether you have the qualities that successful salespeople demonstrate in their real estate careers.

Your Ideal Job

Start with your expectations. Use the categories in Figure 2.1 to describe your ideal job. At this point, do not consider income or any investment you may need to get into the field. Now, match the attributes of real estate sales to the description of your ideal job.

Independence Real estate salespeople are really on their own, creating their own weekly schedules, finding their own business, marketing themselves and budgeting their expenses. In fact, the best way to look at the business is to consider that you are starting your own business under the "umbrella" of a broker. You have little hour-by-hour supervision. Only four to eight hours per week (if that many) are prescheduled for you. People who have planned, organized, budgeted for and managed other businesses find that the skills they developed in their previous businesses are directly transferable to real estate. Have you had previous experience in business planning, budgeting and management (including self-management)?

High Earning Capability Real estate agents can earn very large incomes through persistent hard work, building their careers over a period of years. However, many real estate agents fail even to earn what is commonly termed minimum wage although they work each day. The difference lies in what they *do* each day—not how many hours they spend at work. This book will show exactly what you must

---

Figure 2.1 Your Ideal Job

---

1. **Hours**
   - Regular hours (No weekends or nights. You like time restrictions.) or
   - Irregular hours (Like to finish a project, will work weekends, nights, if needed.)
   - Number of hours willing to work per week: _____

2. **Time Frame**
   - Regular days off and vacation or
   - You name your schedule (Could work 14 days in a row, if needed, to accomplish a goal.)

3. **Amount of Independence**
   - Supervised work with task completion expectations or
   - Unsupervised work, little evaluation or feedback from management

4. **Salary**
   - Steady increase based on cost of living or
   - No salary (Your work determines your income.)

5. **Income Potential**
   - Limited or
   - Unlimited

6. **Risk/Security**
   - Low risk (job security) or
   - High risk (In income—low risk of getting "fired")

7. **Comfort**
   - Little interference with private life or
   - Private life can be put on hold to achieve goal

8. **Working Tasks or People**
   - Like working tasks or
   - Like working with people

9. **Work Environment**
   - Working with a group or
   - Working alone

10. **Planning**
    - Like plan worked out for you or
    - Plan alone to achieve personal goals

FIGURE 2.2 Self-Analysis: Attributes for Success

Rate yourself a 3 if you feel this particular attribute is a real strength of yours; 2 if you feel you're adequate; and 1 if you feel it's not one of your best qualities.

1. I do things on my own; nobody has to tell me to get going. 1 2 3
2. I finish what I start, even if it takes me more time and effort than I thought it would. 1 2 3
3. I'll tackle the challenging activities fast—I like to put myself in the action. 1 2 3
4. I'm the one who plans the get-together; people look to me to organize activities. 1 2 3
5. I have accomplished things that others said I couldn't do; I knew I could. 1 2 3
6. People depend on me because I follow through on a promise. 1 2 3
7. I learn from others I respect; I put that information to use quickly. 1 2 3
8. I get excited about accomplishing something, and this causes me to keep going. 1 2 3
9. I can handle rejection without becoming devastated, because I know it's not personal. 1 2 3
10. I've created ways to do things, and have done them, even when I didn't have lots of information. 1 2 3

---

do to make lots of money in real estate. You decide whether you are willing to do those activities.

Low Barrier of Entry Real estate sales requires a relatively small initial investment. One can get into the field quickly. So, it is an attractive alternative to buying a business franchise or going to school to prepare to enter a profession. The income stream, though, is not immediate. It builds up throughout the first year, as the new agent's expenses continue. Do you have the financial means to support your career for the first few months?

Opportunity for Career Advancement Some real estate sales-people make more money in sales than real estate managers and owners make. However, there are opportunities to go into management, training and marketing, as well as the opportunity to own your own company. If you are willing to do the consistent, sales-generating activities that create strong careers, there are many opportunities for related careers. The last chapter will discuss opportunities and future real estate sales trends.

Do the attractive attributes of real estate match your ideal career? Do the considerations within this discussion give you a better idea of the meaning behind the words? By being honest with yourself about these considerations, you can make a better career decision.

Do You Have the Qualities of Successful Salespeople?

There is probably no field more individualized than real estate sales. There are as many approaches to the business as there are people in the business. Yet, there are certain qualities that are common to successful salespeople. To know whether your strengths match these qualities, complete the self-inventory in Figure 2.2.

Characteristics of Successful Salespeople

Now compare your evaluation of yourself with the qualities successful real estate salespeople demonstrate through their behavior in real estate life. The behavior described in your first question demonstrates *high personal initiative,* the first quality discussed in the following list. Each quality corresponds to the number on the evaluation you just completed above.

1. *High Personal Initiative* In a salaried job, someone gives you a schedule, expectations and time frames. The manager checks your work to be sure you finished it with a certain level of quality. In real estate your manager generally does not become involved in scheduling your activities, checking that you completed those activities or evaluating your work. Successful salespeople become

their own managers from the start, planning their weekly schedule and motivating themselves to just do it.

As a new agent, no one told me what to do. In fact, I had only a part-time manager. I was really independent! The manager's approach could be characterized by an old rhyme: "Here's your desk and here's your phone, good luck son, you're on your own." Any questions? Ask me. Ha! I didn't even *know* the questions—much less the answers! So, I came into the office and hung around. I watched agents previewing lots of homes daily. They knew all the inventory. But they seldom showed homes to buyers. I had to make money, so I didn't follow "the rules" of the office. I decided that to *sell* homes, you had to *show them to buyers*—not just look at them yourself. I showed and sold three homes that first month—even before I knew all the inventory! The people in my office were displeased; how dare I sell something before I knew all the properties available? I apologized and kept selling homes. Later I wondered why I had to know all the inventory to be qualified to sell a home. Who made those rules? (Beware of "rule makers" in any office. They can inhibit you from starting fast in real estate.) If you don't have high personal initiative, you can get stuck hanging around—following the advice of people in the office—who might be playing by different rules.

2. *Tenacity* Since no one (except you) checks with you to see if you call customers back, keep your promises and finish what you start, you must exhibit great tenacity in your work. As you talk to people to get prospects, you will hear no more than yes. The ability to bounce back and keep going until you reach the desired outcome is paramount to your real estate success. I have observed how quickly new agents can become disappointed in themselves. Successful salespeople remember that *tenacity always wins*. Real estate sales people don't get paid for their time. They get paid for their *results*—selling homes and listing homes that sell.

Agents get depressed and discouraged if they don't sell their first home quickly—especially if a friend, also new to the business, sells one first. John had been in the business only three weeks. He had finished his initial training program, which included high numbers of prospecting calls. His friend Sally, in the same program, had just sold a home. While I was having lunch with John, he mentioned he was depressed because he hadn't sold a home (three weeks—and he's depressed already?). I told him if he was really that soft, he should quit now. The next day John sold a home. Long-term real estate sales success can't be measured in terms of weeks.

3. *Risk Taker* Agents who jump right in and start finding prospects, even though they don't have all the real estate knowledge they think they need, have a much better chance of making money before their savings run out. They will tackle the biggest challenges fast, because they are willing to take a risk, fail—and learn.

   Even though Tim wasn't sure exactly how to fill the blanks, he completed an offer to purchase his first week in the business. He had to make some corrections, and was a little embarrassed about it, but chalked it up to a learning experience. With this attitude, Tim sold 14 homes in 4 months. In contrast, some agents wait to write an offer to purchase until they know everything about these agreements but, by the time they feel comfortable, they have forgotten lots of important information. Use it or lose it.

4. *Accountability to Yourself* Planning your week, working your plan and measuring the results of your plan ensure your success. Agents quickly learn that managers really do leave agents alone to be independent. So, some agents spend the first weeks of their career trying to figure out what to do. Then they get scared to do it! So they procrastinate, seeking comfort in organizational activities. Months with no results pass quickly. I have watched this pattern over and over.

   Joan decided to prospect by calling on people in a certain geographical area (commonly called *farming*). She spent five months organizing information and researching the area. By the time she got ready to knock on a door, her savings were depleted. Doing what is safe or easy in real estate sales can quickly destroy your savings account.

5. *Belief in Oneself* It may take you one week, one month or several months to sell your first home (Chapter 9 shows how to ensure a fast start). Your belief in your ability to meet new challenges will tide you over when things go wrong much more that they go right.

Kathy was only 22 when she started selling real estate. It was challenging at first, as she learned how to dress and talk to assure older people she was trustworthy and competent. But Kathy's strong belief in herself carried her to great success. After three years in the business, she attained recognition in the top 10 percent of her 500-agent company! "When the going gets tough, the tough get going" characterizes successful real estate salespeople.

6. *Reliability to Others* Have people told you that they knew they could always rely on you? Reliability is so important to real estate success. Your customers and clients will ask themselves, "Is he reliable?" "Can I trust her?" They will draw their conclusions by remembering whether you kept your promises. Building trust and confidence with the public is a series of kept promises, each small individually, but adding up to a value judgment about the individual. In the National Association of REALTORS® Horizon report, the public rated trustworthiness as the most important attribute consumers want in a real estate agent.

7. *Willingness To Learn* When you start something new, do you argue with the person teaching you about how to do it? Do you resist new ideas? Do you critique every idea? Do you resist getting into action? If so, look carefully at entering real estate. It is a performance business, not a knowledge endeavor. What is needed is willingness to accept an idea, while reserving judgment, and *try it out.* The successful salesperson grasps an idea, tries it out and then forms a judgment. The unsuccessful agent decides why the idea will not work and feels no need to do anything.

Denny was a successful coach. Coaches know that high performance starts by practicing simple skills. Children find this easy. Adults resist it; they want to make everything complex. But, having a childlike approach to anything new is very important. Denny's childlike approach to coaching and life worked for him in real estate. For his enthusiasm and willingness to try new ideas without negating them helped him create innovative personal marketing strategies. Unlike many agents who spend most of their time criticizing others' activities, Denny tried new strategies—and then refined them. In three years, Denny built a fabulous business based on long-term customer satisfaction.

8. *Enthusiasm* Getting excited about an idea is the best short-term motivation for the new agent. When I interview a potential agent, and find that I am not sure which one of us is asleep, I question the person's short-term motivation to get into the business. Enthusiasm helps us throw ourselves into the task, to look at challenges as possibilities, to accept not knowing everything and just do something. The public rates enthusiasm as *one of the three most important qualities* in choosing a real estate agent.

9. *Handling Rejection* Sales is a business where no is heard more than yes. Our ability to accept no and keep going is key to sales success. Most people in sales give up too easily. An AT&T survey of their salespeople found that most salespeople gave up after the first no. But 80 percent of the public say no five times before they say yes. So, one salesman out of ten makes 80 percent of the sales. Through sales activities, I found that buyers say no many times before they say yes. This habit is just human nature.

   During my first year in real estate, my boss was helping me prepare and present an offer. He told me to take three nos before I left the negotiating table. As I presented the offer, I quickly got three nos. But I knew the sellers should sell the home to these buyers. So, I started counting the nos on my fingers. After I got to ten nos (and used all my fingers), I got a yes! I also discovered the fun of going through the process to get to yes—and getting paid more often.

10. *Creativity* The nineties are an era of constant change, of turbulent markets and increased competition. To stay ahead of the game, agents must keep changing and creating new sales strategy. I don't mean that you must be a creative marketing genius. Merely have fun with new ideas and implement some of them to ensure your success. Poor agents look for the guaranteed one way that always works. They spend their time judging others, not doing. Successful agents have an attitude like Denny's. They learn creative concepts and apply them to their businesses. That is truly the one way that always works.

A few years ago, personal promotion was just starting to be popular for real estate agents. Because I had just hired three new agents, I decided to help them promote themselves. All of them created great brochures and other strategies, while some experienced agents in the office spent their energies telling the new agents why personal promotion would not work. Who made more money that year? Of course, the new agents. And they kept refining and changing their promotional strategy as other agents started discovering it. Now, one of those agents is so successful she is asked to share her multimillion dollar success in national presentations.

Figure 2.3, shown on page 30, lists qualities I value—qualities I have observed in "winners." This list is used in interviewing to match the interviewee to the ideal salesperson.

What about People Skills?

In the seventies and early eighties, real estate salespeople relied on maintaining social relationships with their clientele to create business and the real estate market took care of the rest. Now, with more sophisticated consumers and competitive real estate salespeople, maintaining social relationships is not enough. Consumers expect salespeople to be business people. And, the market doesn't always do what the agents want it to do for them. For example, in the seventies, agents regularly took overpriced listings to please sellers. Inflation would sooner or later drive home prices up. The overpriced property would become well priced and would sell. Unfortunately, agents continued using this appeasement strategy in the eighties in a depressed, declining market. Of course, overpriced homes did not sell. Predictably the sellers blamed the agent, and the relationship was destroyed. In the nineties, listing overpriced properties creates *customer dissatisfaction*. In a *Consumer Reports* survey, sellers said they were satisfied with an agent's service only if their home sold in a short period of time at close to listed price. The age of appeasement is long gone. So, in the nineties liking people must be tempered with good, sound business decisions.

Top Producer's Profile   I am always curious about success. Why do some people make a success of something, while others, seemingly as talented, fail? It is not what they *are,* it is what they *do.* Studying the behaviors of multimillion-dollar-producing salespeople makes it possible to draw a profile of a top producer. A study by the University of Illinois found that top producers

- were self-starters;
- had high energy;
- worked more days and weekends than average producers;
- worked more hours and evenings;
- were intensely task-oriented;
- took part in relatively little social conversation on the job;
- completed more face-to-face contacts;
- had high standards for prospects (qualified them stringently before they would put buyers in the car or go to listing presentations);
- had high client candor (frankly told them the truth, even if the client didn't want to hear it); and
- needed recognition more than security.

Good news for new agents: The researchers found that *experience beyond one year was a nonsignificant factor to high productivity.* This means it is possible to build a dynamic career in real estate quickly—if you demonstrate the behaviors listed here.

The ASPIRE Questionnaire   So far, this chapter has investigated the qualities and behavior one needs to succeed in real estate sales. Besides the informal self-analysis questionnaire provided here, there are various personality and sales profiles available for your use. One was created especially to predict success in real estate sales: ASPIRE, a computerized questionnaire developed by Life Insurance Marketing and Research Association (LIMRA), a nonprofit trade association of the insurance industry. From LIMRA's job analysis of 800 successful real estate associates, these qualities emerged:

- Energetic
- Mature
- Responsible
- Well organized

Figure 2.3 Qualities of a Successful Real Estate Associate

- **High Personal Initiative**

  Your success depends on your being able to create programs and implement them on your own, with relatively little monitoring.

- **Tenacity**

  Only those who stick with it will win. Plan on dedicating one year to establishing your business.

- **Mental Toughness**

  A positive mental attitude is essential. Those who give up easily will try to influence the tenacious, mentally tough individual to give up. It takes courage to keep going in this long-term business.

- **Belief in Oneself**

  We each have to know, inside ourselves, that we are capable, that we have the talent and the tenacity to succeed and must be able to depend on ourselves.

- **Willingness To Take Direction**

  Real estate is a constantly changing field. Those who win learn new skills and apply them consistently.

- **Enthusiasm**

  A joy in doing and a desire to accomplish shows itself in an enthusiastic attitude.

- **Creativity**

  In today's marketing-oriented world, an agent must be creative enough to design programs where he or she stands out as valuable and different.

- **Educated and Communicative**

  Writing skills are a necessity today. Effective verbal communication is also important to success. Our customers and clients expect good communication skills.

- **Team Player**

  The preservation of office spirit and cooperation is very important. We are all more successful together.

- Interacts well with others
- Dedicated to a career in real estate
- Has contacts in the community

The questions asked in ASPIRE are about a person's actual behavior. ASPIRE is based on the premise that the way people behaved in the past predicts how they will behave in the future. Here's a sample question: In the past, were you ever responsible for a number of other people's welfare? Your answer demonstrates your degree of responsibility—one of the attributes of a successful salesperson.

ASPIRE has proven to be a valuable tool in helping real estate companies make good hiring decisions. Behavioral profiles such as ASPIRE are likely to take on greater importance in real estate in the 1990s. As you interview, take advantage of opportunities to complete a profile questionnaire. What you learn about your style will help you in your sales career.

How Your Background Affects Your Real Estate Success

A group of managers discuss the type of people they like and don't like to hire: "I *love* teachers. They're so helpful–and they're great communicators." "Beware of hiring someone who's retired military. They're used to structure and telling *others* what to do." "I don't hire any new agents I need to train. I like to hire only experienced agents." "I never hire people unless they've worked at least three different jobs."

Every manager has his or her preferences. Generally, managers hire people like themselves. But, everyone brings pluses and minuses from earlier life to real estate sales. Looking at backgrounds can reveal how these influences help—and challenge—one's chances of real estate success.

Nurturers: Teachers, Social Workers, Home Managers These people went into these professions because they enjoy helping people. With that attitude, they can be a huge success in real estate. But, watch out. They may be willing to knock on doors for a good cause, but are they willing to ask people to buy for *their* cause? Are they tough enough to handle sales rejection? Are they tough enough to take six nos to get a yes? Frequently people from these fields find that they get walked all over, and then they either get tough or get out of the business. I can spot a *nurturer*. A nurturer doesn't want "salesperson" on business cards and fears that people won't like him or her if they know he or she wants to sell them something. And, nurturers do not like the connotations of the word salesperson (that is, *their connotations*). To get over this, nurturers must convince themselves that *sales is a valuable service*. They have to convince themselves, too, that it is in the customer's best interest to work with them because of their nurturing traits. Nurturers also need to keep their eyes on the goal: selling the home. They can get lost in service to people and forget to finish the task. Nurturers need to find a supportive, firm environment with a manager who understands their strengths and needs—one who will lovingly push them out the door. "Tough love" works here.

To succeed, nurturers must be able to move

- from empathy → to → ego (think more of themselves and less of others) and
- from people → to → tasks (focus more on getting the job done).

Controllers: Managers, Attorneys, Retired Military—People Who Have Been in Positions of Authority Controllers like to tell people what to do—and expect them to do it! With that take-charge attitude, they can do well in real estate sales. They have no trouble telling people to buy. They just order them to do it—fast. And if the customer doesn't buy, they get frustrated. So they must learn to *back off*. Now, they're no longer the boss. Now, there is much less structure to hang onto—and to hold others to. Now, they must develop several latent qualities: One is patience.

A fellow in our office who owned several companies and took early retirement is a controller. He likes to cut corners and *close* but he cannot figure out why his customers do not do as he says. In fact, he loses customers because they say he is pushy. As you might guess, I am a controller. When I went into real estate and found I had so much to learn, I felt out of control. I got angry and frustrated; I lost patience; I came home at night, yelled at my family and threw pots and pans. I hated not knowing all the answers. I always felt embarrassed. My most used phrase seemed to be, "I don't know, but I'll find out." The only way I learned a little patience was that I became fascinated with sales—with the ability to "control" a sales situation (my nickname was "the velvet sledgehammer"). Controllers who slow down and consider their customer's needs find that the game of sales becomes fun. They are in control but much more subtly than before. To succeed, a controller needs a manager who sets firm guidelines, lays out a simple plan and gives lots of praise for results. A last word from one controller to another: Become childlike. Look at real estate sales as a new adventure. As a "babe in the woods," you can enhance some of your other qualities but need to redevelop to be successful in your new career.

To succeed in real estate sales, controllers must move

- from ego → to → empathy (pay more attention to customers/clients) and
- from tasks → to → people (pace the flow of the sales process to your customer's needs).

Promoters: Marketers, Salespeople They have it all, right? They're good talkers, they're flashy, they're outgoing—the epitome of the salesperson. It is true that people in sales/promotion have valuable skills and traits. They understand the sales process and, characteristically have a great personality—they love people. They *can* be great successes in real estate sales. But, they, too, have challenges. They love people so much that they do not want to tell them bad news. They hate rejection and take it personally. My husband is a perfect promoter-type. As a radio personality and disk jockey, he charmed thousands of people. They loved him and were drawn to him and he responded warmly. But, in a situation where bad news must be conveyed, guess who conveys it? You bet—me, the controller! Promoters must learn to give bad news and be able to risk rejection. Otherwise, promoters get known as slippery salespeople!

"Sally should go into real estate, she's a good talker." I hear people suggest that regularly. But, sales requires excellent *listening* skills, not talking skills. Especially today. Customers don't want to be talked into buying. They want information, counseling and help with the decision-making process. They want to be listened to. Some of the best salespeople I have ever known were the quietest.

As a new agent, I marveled at Bob, a salesperson who held new homes open. He made a great deal of money but he was very quiet. One day, I visited him at his open house and heard the magic. He greeted a couple at the door, brought them inside, and started *asking questions*. He seemed so interested in what those customers had to say. They seemed to love talking about themselves. Through his questioning techniques, Bob found out everything he needed to know to help them. I could see that Bob had mastered the skill of *active listening* and applied it to real estate sales. He didn't dump loads of information on them to show he knew what he was doing. Through his questioning procedures, he controlled the conversation. At the end of their visit, he had an appointment to see their present home. They thanked him profusely for his help.

New agents who are talkers can talk their way right out of forming a relationship with prospects. The old saying is true: "Customers don't care what you know until they know you care." Do not underestimate the practice it takes to master the skill of active listening. If you're a talker, take a skill-developing sales course such as the Dale Carnegie Sales Course. Otherwise, you can talk your way out of real estate success.

Promoters need a manager they can talk to. They need a reasonable structure to form their day and keep them on track. They need enough support to withstand rejection and do the hard things, such as taking no and giving out the bad news.

Promoters must move

- from empathy → to → ego (toughen up to take rejection) and
- from people → to → tasks (don't get diverted from the goal).

Task-Oriented People: Accountants, Engineers   Years ago, people who liked tasks more than people were discouraged from going into sales fields. But, with the technical knowledge required today, the increased paperwork load and the attention to detail needed to provide good customer service, the task-oriented person can do well in real estate sales. They also have challenges. Because they tend to look at real estate sales as tasks to be completed, task-oriented people will grasp a list of tasks and continue doing tasks even if they are not getting results. They forget that the goal is to make money. They must be helped to analyze the list of tasks, to measure results and revise the task list to ensure results. Most important, they must develop people skills. For most of their lives, they have gotten results by doing the task. It is difficult for them to focus on the people. So, they must think about the sales process as a *group of tasks that involves people.* Otherwise, they will hide in the paperwork, filing, collating and recording. To get out of that rut, they will have to be self motivated.

George began his real estate sales career at the age of 26. He was extremely shy, had few people skills, but was a wonderful organizer. He loved tasks. He began his real estate career as many of us did, with little guidance. He sold only one home his first year. But, as a task-oriented person, he was very patient and looked at long-term results. He found that, for him, getting to know people in a geographical area to become their *resident specialist* was a task he liked to perform. Slowly and steadily his business grew . Realizing he needed people skills to increase his results, he learned to engage people. Because of his tenacity and high motivation to succeed, he became a top agent, among the top 2 percent of agents in earnings nationally. One of the reasons he has created such a strong business is that he dots all his i's and crosses the t's. His care with the details has gained him long-term customer loyalty. They can count on George.

A task-oriented person needs to find a manager who will provide a detailed, proven business-producing plan, and who will work closely with the new agent to monitor and analyze activities and results. That way, the task-oriented person can realize monetary results and avoid doing tasks that do not lead to results.

Task-oriented people must move

- from ego → to → empathy (learn to consider the differences in people) and
- from tasks → to → people.

Real Estate Sales As Your First Career

As you graduate from high school or college, you are considering real estate as a career. Is it a good career for a young person? *Yes.* More and more recent graduates have chosen real estate sales. Why? High income potential, "ownership," and related investment opportunities. It is a good career choice if you are mature, capable of accepting lots of responsibility and are willing to look at sales as a long-term commitment. There are certain things you can do to gain acceptance with customers. One is to dress conservatively. Another is to drive a conservative car and drive conservatively. You must communicate that you are serious, understanding and capable of helping people with the largest investment most people will ever make: a home. You bring lots of great qualities to real estate:

- Enthusiasm
- Energy (without it, you can't maintain the hours needed to launch your career)
- Creativity (being willing to try new things)
- Willing to take direction
- Better-educated than your predecessors

This is a major trend in real estate sales: people are making real estate their *first* career choice. With the excellent educational and training programs available today, I strongly encourage young people to consider real estate sales seriously.

Working with Your Spouse

Husband-wife teams can be very successful. It is another partnership. The key is to decide on the duties each will perform before starting to work together. Read the description of personality styles. Which one are you? Which one is your spouse? Which real estate activities will each of you enjoy doing? Can you divide your duties to match your styles and strengths? Strong, true partnerships work best when both agents do their individual businesses and help each other in time crunches.

This works beautifully in my office. Charles and Marion Deardorff are both very successful salespeople. They were in the business as individuals several years before they married. They co-list homes together, telling sellers that the sellers are getting twice the service for the same cost. However, to maximize their earnings, they sell homes individually. When one of them gets in a pinch, the other helps out. This arrangement works because they really work at it a true partnership.

However, here's how most partnerships work. One person sells while the other person does the paperwork. That arrangement is not called a selling partnership. It is a salesperson working with an assistant, a trend of the nineties.

Here is a way to determine which kind of arrangement you should consider. If one of you enjoys paperwork, organization and follow-up— the *support* activities—that person becomes the assistant. While teaching one of my business planning classes, I was impressed with a student, who was well organized, perceptive and supportive (we instructors love these people). She told me she was her husband's assistant, and was there to get him organized! For some, that works. My husband jokes that I have organized and managed hundreds of people but, in twenty years of marriage, I haven't made any progress with him.

There is no right or wrong working arrangement. An in any relationship, it is the misunderstandings that destroy any kind of partnership. If you think any kind of spouse partnership is for you, find some people in selling partnerships and in assistant partnerships. Ask them how they have made a success of these arrangements. When you interview, ask managers their opinion about partnerships and how they handle them in their offices (desk space, commissions, etc.).

Summary

This chapter investigates the traits and qualities that successful salespeople demonstrate daily in their careers, the challenges each type of career-changer faces, the strengths each one brings to the business, and the type of management help each group needs to succeed.

In closing this chapter, finish your internal review by answering these questions:

- Do you see yourself more clearly now as a real estate salesperson? If so, in what ways?
- What qualities do you see demonstrated in your life that will assist you in real estate sales?
- What do you think will be your biggest challenges?
- What kind of office, management, and support systems will benefit you?

Save the information from the last two questions for your interview. You will want to ask interview questions to find the particular manager and office to help you optimize your strengths and meet your specific challenges.

3 Your Activities on the Job

"Boy, what I would have given to have had a job description indicating a plan of attack. For example, this is how your day must be scheduled: prospecting, three hours, follow-up, clerical, etc."

—Rick Franz, formerly in the restaurant management business

In This Chapter . . . .

- Your job description for success
- An agent's life—on and off the job
- A new agent's daily activities
- How to have a life outside real estate
- Life beyond "new"
- As your business develops

. . . .

Daily Activities—Not Hours Spent— Add Up to Sales

After interviewing hundreds of potential agents, I can predict the most-asked questions. This is one of the most common: "How much time do I have to devote daily to become successful?"

Unlike salaried positions, real estate agents are not paid for the number of hours they are on the job. They are paid for their results. But, because most new agents come from salaried positions, where working the required number of hours ensured being retained as employees, it is difficult for them to grasp the concept that to be successful in real estate, *business-producing activities must be performed until the desired results are attained.* It is not how long you are on the job, it is what you do that determines your income, and you must *do* it—even if it takes much longer than you expected—if your goal is a *result* in terms of sales! Think of this the way you think about remodeling your home. You start the project estimating it will take three months. After three months, you are half-finished (I know, I lived through it!). But, because your goal is a *finished* remodel, you continue the job until you get the result you want. You understand the concept—but, what does this mean a new agent has to do each day to become successful? Approximately how long will it take a new agent to do it?

Even though time on the job does not guarantee success, there are some general time requirements that are essential to create a successful career. According to the National Association of REALTORS®, a REALTOR® works an average of 42 hours a week. New agents will tell you, though, that they spend 45 to 60 hours a week their first year because they are learning their jobs—and more effective ways to do their jobs. Just as you would not want to stop in the middle of a fascinating project, new agents find they love spending long hours establishing their careers. They want to conquer the challenges they face as new agents—and they are willing to devote the time necessary to establish a great career.

The Essentials of the Job

Chapter 2 compared the activities agents *can* do with the critical, or essential activities they *must* do to get a paycheck. Look at these essential activities as a *sales path*. Figure 3.1 shows the activities agents do every day to start and journey on this sales path to success.

Paths lead to destinations. When you wander off a path, you may find interesting diversions, but it takes longer to reach your destination. When you stay on the sales path, doing these activities consistently, you can make money—fast. The more activities you complete off the path (Figure 3.2) while doing fewer activities on the path, the less money you make in a given period of time.

Figure 3.1   Essential Activities on the Sales Path

These activities are important as support to sales-producing activities. But, done in excess, they replace sales path activities. There is only so much anyone can do in a business day. Successful agents prioritize and control the number and type of activities they perform.

Figure 3.2   Activities Off the Sales Path

- Education
- Organizing files
- Having coffee with the gang at the office
- Creating mailers
- Previewing properties
- Attending meetings
- Critiquing another's business
- Following up with transactions
- Marketing a listing (not face-to-face)

A Job Description for Success

Creating a successful real estate career is not a matter of doing all the activities that a real estate agent can do. Instead, success in real estate sales requires

1. doing the essential activities often, at top priority; and
2. doing support activities as needed to prepare for and continue essential activities.

Plan Ahead Usually, when we follow a path or take a trip, we have to reach our destination within a certain time frame, or our money and time run out. In creating real estate sales careers, the same is true. Too many side trips doing support activities fill time that could have been devoted to sales path activities. By the time we realize our money is running out, we are out of time to create a career.

The job description for agents in my office is in Figure 3.3. See how it describes and prioritizes real estate activities. To ensure a new agent's success, I hire only those who understand this job description and agree to do the work described here.

Jump-Start Your Sales Cycle For Success Another way to look at real estate sales activities is to show them as a sales cycle. Smart new agents jump-start the sales cycle by going right out, talking to lots of people and asking for business. Think of it this way: The business *starts* when you start talking to people. (See Figure 3.4.)

Schedule for a Careerist

Figure 3.5, shown on page 45, is a prototype weekly schedule that will create a careerist income, an income that is substantial and quick to come. Note that about half your day, or about four hours, is spent in generating business, that is, prospecting, or going out to find potential customers and clients. This includes activities such as knocking on doors; telephone canvassing; calling on people you know to ask for leads; calling on FSBOs (for sale by owners); and calling expired listings (listings that have not sold during the term of the listing). Other activities take second priority to prospecting activities.

Figure 3.3 Job Description for a Successful Real Estate Agent

---

Sales associates consistently perform three categories of activities:
1. **Find Prospects**
   - *Create a business plan* to identify certain prospects in particular markets.
   - Make many sales calls (100 per week for the first month).

Agents' income and fast success are determined by the number of people contacted consistently in specific target markets.

2. **Generate Sales Activities (as result of business plan)**
   - Showing homes to qualified customers
   - Listing marketable properties that sell in normal market time

3. **Goal: Often Do the Activities That Guarantee a Commission Check**
   - Selling a home
   - Listing sold

Preparation and support activities include the following (do these only to support high-priority sales activities):

   - Preview properties
   - Paperwork/sales follow-up
   - Education
   - Meetings, etc.

By working an aggressive, personally tailored business plan, associates ensure early income and long-term success.

A Day In the Life of a New-Agent Careerist

To get even closer to a new agent's real-life daily activity, let's join Marie Smith, a determined, dedicated agent, as she works through a typically scheduled day. First, a little background about Marie, so you understand the skills she brought to real estate and the challenges facing her as a new agent. Marie was a high school English teacher who became a salesperson, selling hotel convention space. She moved 2,000 miles to the Seattle area just before entering real estate. Even without a background in real estate, she feels good about her sales

Figure 3.4 Sales Cycle

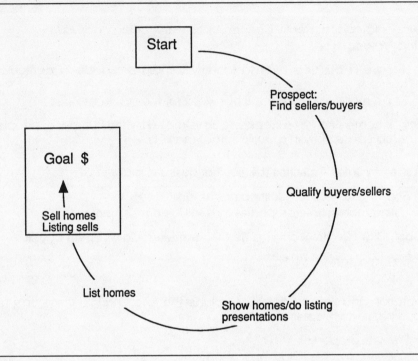

and writing skills because she developed these skills in her former jobs.

Marie goes to the office at 7 AM because she knows she needs to plan activities and do paperwork and research while it is quiet there. She spends one hour in support activities. Because she was in sales, where she had to go out and generate leads, she knows that a sales job starts there. Her goal is to spend four hours per day, contacting 100 potential leads per week. She knows those time frames and contact numbers will give her the number of potential clients and customers she needs to meet her earning expectations (she intends to sell a home within a month).

By 8 AM, she is ready to phone potential buyers and sellers, to ask whether or not they know someone who wants to buy or sell a home. Marie chose to phone them because she knows few people in the area, and realizes that this is a quick method to find prospects. From 8 AM

Figure 3.5 Prototype Schedule for the New Agent

TIME COMMITMENTS: How to allocate your time to ensure quick success

Activity	Daily	No./Week	Hours
Prospecting	4 hours	5 days	20
Open houses		once a week	3–4
Floor time		1 day	3
Business meetings	1 hour	once a week	1
Office education	1 hour	1 day	1
Mgr./Agent counseling		once a week	1–2
*Previewing	2 hours	5 days	10

*(only until you're comfortable with the inventory. Then cut back on the hours)

SCHEDULE

Mon.	8:00–8:45	Meet w/Mgr. Paperwork/ Calls	Tues.	Day off	TAKE IT!
	8:45–9:30	Business meeting			
	9:30–12:30	New office listing tour			
	Lunch				
	1:30–5:30	Prospect			
Wed.	8:00–9:00	Paperwork	Thurs.	8:00–9:00	Paperwork
	9:00–10:00	Prospect		9:00–10:00	Preview properties
	10:00–12:00	Preview properties		12:00–3:00	Floor time or buyer tour
	1:00–5:00	Prospect		3:00–6:00	Prospect
Fri.	8:00–8:45	Paperwork	Sat.	9:00–12:00	Prospect
	8:45–9:30	Office class		1:00–4:00	Listing presentation or buyer tour
	9:30–12:00	Preview properties			
	1:00–5:00	Prospect		4:00–5:00	Paperwork
	7:00–8:00	Listing presentation			
Sun.	12:00–2:00	Prospect			
	2:00–5:00	Open house or buyer tour			
	5:00–6:00	Listing presentation			

*Reprinted with permission of Windermere Real Estate, Seattle, Washington.

to 10 AM, Marie talks to 40 homeowners, and gets two appointments for that week (about normal for Marie—one or two out of 40).

At 10 AM, Marie takes a break and goes to support activities. In order to counsel buyers and sellers well, she wants to be sure she knows the properties available on the market. So, for two hours, Marie previews properties in her area—but not the way noncareerists preview them. Because she has customers and clients, she looks at properties for a specific purpose. In fact, each support activity that Marie does, is related to real customers and clients. At noon, Marie takes a break and has a sandwich at a sandwich shop near where she lives and works. While there, she hands her card to the waitress and asks for prospects. The waitress refers a friend who wants to buy a property.

At 1 PM, Marie continues her business-generating activities by knocking on doors in the neighborhood where she lives. A home has been listed there by an agent in her office; with permission from that agent and seller, she tells the neighbors about the new listing—and asks for prospects. In order to promote herself, Marie has created a brochure describing the newly listed property including a section about herself. To optimize the effect of these calls, Marie plans to go back into this neighborhood later to tell the neighbors more about this property (an open house, price reduction, listing sold, etc.) Marie knows that it takes several meetings with someone before they will remember her, and trust her enough to give her leads or do business with her themselves. She is establishing herself as a *property expert* in her own neighborhood because she knows that people want to buy and sell real estate with someone they know and trust. In two hours, Marie knocks on 50 doors and finds 20 homeowners at home. Some of these people already know Marie. One is interested in chatting further with her about selling his home within the next three months. Marie makes an appointment to meet with him and his wife later that week. Now past 3:30 PM, it is time for Marie to head back to the office to return phone calls, handle paperwork, and do other support activities.

She finishes by 5 PM, and gets ready to go home. As she gets up from her desk, she receives a phone call. An agent has an offer on Marie's listed property and wants to present the offer that evening. Marie calls home to tell her 15-year-old son that she will not be home for dinner. She asks her son to relay that message to her husband; Marie has taught both men to cook and they have been very supportive of Marie's dedication to her new career. As you know, Marie's goal is to sell a home within a month—so she can get a check by month four. So, she started the business cycle by *prospecting aggressively*. That does not mean she was overly aggressive towards the people she talked to; it just means she aggressively pursued her plan. By the way, this is a true story. I hired Marie and helped her create and complement her business plan. By following this aggressive plan, Marie made over $85,000 her first year in real estate. Marie credits her success to two things: (1) She created and implemented a business development plan with large contact numbers and (2) applied her sales skills to real estate.

Marie's Business Development Plan   You have read the description of a typical day in the life of Marie Smith, careerist. In order for Marie to know what to do every day, she had to first build an initial *business development plan*. Here is how Marie built her plan for her first three months in the business:

1. Marie decided on the results she wanted: number of sales and listings.
2. Marie figured out the number of buyer showings and listing presentations she needed to complete in her first month to reach her goals.
3. Because I (as her manager) told her that 100 contacts a week would assure her the number of buyers and sellers she needed to reach her sales goals, Marie penciled this number in her daily planner (20 calls per day, five days per week).

Figure 3.6 shows Marie's business development plan, expressed as her sales path to success.

It is simply a numbers game, isn't it? I keep statistics on the ratios of activities to results, so I can help people like Marie put the numbers into the plan. I also help agents choose the markets from which they will get their business, design the specific initial contact method and create materials and systems for follow-up contacts. In your interview process, ask to see the business development planning system that the manager will use to guide you as you begin your career. Ask the manager how he or she will serve as your business consultant.

Have a Life

One of a new agent's fears is that he or she will not have a life outside real estate. That need not be the case. You don't have to be available all the time. If you have enough good, qualified customers and clients, you can refer the leads you cannot handle, or do not want to handle. You can even refuse to show homes on your day off and refer the customer to someone else. In a trade-off arrangement, you can ask an agent partner to go to a purchase presentation on one of your listings when you are unavailable.

Here is the key to planning your time to include days off: When you are generating a lot of qualified customers and clients and are on your

---

Figure 3.6 Marie's Sales Path and Business Plan

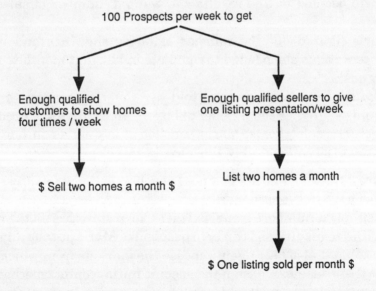

100 Prospects per week to get

Enough qualified customers to show homes four times / week

Enough qualified sellers to give one listing presentation/week

$ Sell two homes a month $

List two homes a month

$ One listing sold per month $

way to fulfilling your income expectations, you muster the intestinal fortitude to turn down potential business or refer it to someone else. Doctors take days off. Accountants take days off. When agents create a careerist business development plan, and consistently work the plan, they create a professional's business. They earn their days off. Still, don't let me kid you. For the first year in the business, you will work more crazy hours, more total hours and more consecutive days in a row than you ever imagined. Why? Because you love the challenge of completing the sales cycle of selling homes and listing homes that sell.

Weekends and Evenings As a new agent, establishing your own independent business, you are truly an entrepreneur. If you were opening your first restaurant on a prayer and a shoestring, you would do everything possible to ensure success. You would be there early in the morning and late at night, doing any job that had to be done to meet your goal: a successful restaurant. It is the same with your real estate career. So, you work weekends to hold open houses, prospect and show homes. On weekends, more buyers are available and both sellers are generally available for listing presentations. For a new agent, not being able to work weekends or refusing to do so, is like opening your restaurant from 5 to 6 AM and from 10 to 12 PM. It may be convenient for you but it surely is not convenient for your diners— and they pay your bills.

For New Agents, Is There Life outside Real Estate? There had better be; otherwise, new agents suffer burnout, that emotional overload from expending a lot of energy with the goal buried in what becomes grinding daily activity. To have a life outside real estate, new agents must establish an effective business development plan. In that schedule, agents must include at least one day off per week. Every six to eight weeks, all agents should schedule three to four days away.

The Importance of Scheduling Free Time For most agents, real estate sales is a completely new and different world, a world we throw ourselves into, immersing ourselves in the curious language, exciting sales cycle, and dismaying, depressing reality of rejection. For many, this immersion also causes us to bury the real self, sometimes to the point of forgetting that we are valuable, knowledgeable, capable human beings. We all need to continue taking part in the activities that give us a sense of ourselves, that remind us of our unique, intrinsic, human value, and share in life beyond real estate. Personally, that meant continuing to play music jobs, even though it resulted in getting about four hours' sleep on the weekends. Holding public open houses at that time was a constant battle against sleep, a battle that I lost a couple of times! However, doing two disparate things at once was very important to my self-esteem. It helped maintain a balance between something I knew very well and something that was completely strange and new.

Take this advice: Schedule a hobby, activity, leisure-time pleasure, visit with friends, take walks, get out of town—whatever you do to enjoy the real you. Be willing to give up some potential income to maintain a sense of balance in your life. You will need it when things get rough.

What about Agent Partnerships To Ease the Load?   Anyone who has ever gone into partnership in a business knows that partnerships create additional management challenges. However, agents do form good partnerships if they clearly define duties for each partner. Two experienced, successful agents in my office formed a partnership when both started traveling extensively. Each knew the others' customers and clients, and would take over all the duties of each others' business when one was gone. Commissions were shared equally.

Most partnerships are not like this one. Usually, one partner is good at getting business and working the customers and clients. The other partner does support work. Actually, a partner who does support duties should be paid as an assistant, not a full partner. Problems in this kind of partnership occur when one partner feels he or she is doing more or more important work than the other. My advice to new agents: Start your own business alone so you will learn all aspects of the business and be forced to concentrate on the critical activities that ensure an income—fast!

How To Keep Your Family While Starting in Real Estate You get the picture. Going into real estate sales is not like taking another salaried job. It is much more like starting your first restaurant—when you are the host, dishwasher, cashier, cook and bookkeeper. Real estate can become a 24-hour-a-day commitment if you let it. And, even if you are careful not to work every day all day, you'll probably be preoccupied thinking about real estate to the exclusion of much else for your first few months in the business. This focus on real estate can be very disruptive to the rhythm of your family life. In addition to scheduling days off and time to be you, it is important that you discuss the nature of your new job with your family. Here are several important steps to take with your spouse, family or other household members:

1. Ask your family to read sections of this book, and discuss the nature of this entrepreneurial job.
2. Discuss a new schedule for home chores with your family, so that different family members prepare meals and otherwise cover tasks you usually perform. You may not be able to do the same chores to the same level of excellence that you did while you were living your prior life.
3. Be sure to build some rewards for members of your family to be given when you reach your goals. Ask yourself, "What's in it for them?" Sit down with your family, decide on rewards and how those rewards are tied to your reaching your goals. Create some mutual goals so that your career becomes part of your family's long-term goals.
4. Explain the nature of this job to your family, what you will do to make money, your time frames for activities and goals and the potential scheduling conflicts that could cut into your family time. Ask each member of your family if they understand your new commitments, and if they are willing to support your efforts.
5. Show your spouse/partner your office and introduce your spouse/partner and manager. Many times, agents leave real estate sales quickly because the spouse neither understands the nature of the job nor is willing to support the activities and erratic time schedule of the new agent. It is very important that your spouse see where and with whom you're going to work and get a

chance to get to know your manager. That way, all the parties can empathize with the stresses that the new agent will experience. The good news: That first paycheck really enhances the spouse's view of your career!

As Your Business Develops

To be successful, you will keep generating prospects actively throughout your career. In that sense, you always follow the new-agent plan. An evolutionary process occurs, though, as you spend more time in the business. As a new agent, if you make 100 contacts per week for your first month, you will find you have generated so much business that you'll have to cut back on your amount of contacts. But, do not stop contacting. Think of prospecting like riding a bicycle. When you stop pedaling, you fall off. By measuring the numbers of contacts you make and the results you get, you will find a happy medium enabling you to generate the leads and income you want— and still have a "life."

Mark, an agent in my office, went through the same patterns many new agents endure. As a new agent, Mark sat around for his first two months in the business, confused about what to do. He found it fascinating and comforting to preview properties and organize his files. As time went by, through, he got frantic because his money was running out, and he had no sales. When I became manager of that office, I immediately found him a *staff advisor*—someone who would jump-start him every day to go out and prospect. Along with his staff adviser, I set up a business development plan for him. I met with Mark every three to seven days. Within a month, Mark had his first sale. In four months, he has had two sales and four listings. Now, he has a new problem—how to juggle all his business! You can bet that's a much better challenge for Mark to have than his first one. By over-loading himself, Mark will learn ways of qualifying, prioritizing and streamlining his business until he finds a pace that delivers the results he wants, consistently.

Business Sources Evolve with Your Business

Experienced agents who maintain successful careers still prospect for potential customers and clients. But, they go to different sources to find that business. The best source of an experienced agent's business is from those people who have previously bought and sold homes through him or her. In Figure 3.7, a pie chart, taken from a study by the National Association of REALTORS® shows that almost half of an agent's business was generated from former customers and clients. This does not mean agents can sit back and wait for the phone to ring. As long as the experienced agent *aggressively keeps in touch with these people*—and asks for leads—he or she can maintain a good income.

Figure 3.7   Experienced Agent's Business Sources

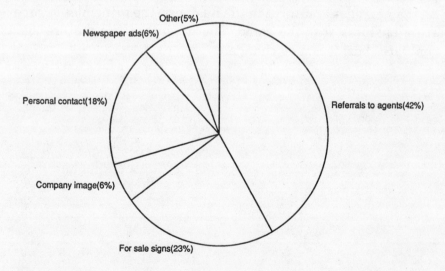

Summary

As a typical day in the life of a new real estate agent was described, how did you feel? Were you excited and challenged by the fact that you could complete activities each day that ensured a check? Did you find yourself trying to reject those activities in favor of research and support activities? Why? What were your family considerations? What challenges might you have there? Overall, how does this practical, everyday picture of a careerist differ from your earlier perceptions?

Chapter 3 shows a typical day in the life of a real estate agent. Important points in this chapter are:

- A careerist's daily plan revolves around a half-day of business-generating activities.
- A careerist creates a business development plan so that he or she knows how many contacts, what kind of contacts and how to create the contacts that ensure reaching the goals quickly. He or she puts measurable activities in daily calendar and completes these activities.
- Family and household members need to be part of the planning process.
- As the new agent matures in the business, the principles of generating business stay the same. The ways that the mature agent generates business may change.

4 How Much Money Can You Make?

"I came into real estate thinking that, with my sales background, I'd make six figures my first year. I had friends in the business, and I just knew I could be as successful as they were! After a few months, I found it was more challenging than I'd imagined. It took me longer to 'learn the ropes' than I thought it would. But I love it! Although I didn't quite break six figures my first year I laid the groundwork for my second year. It's exciting, challenging, hard work."

—Kay Zatine, top first-year salesperson, formerly a radio salesperson.

In This Chapter . . . .

- Real estate incomes—What's really "average"
- Getting out of it what you put in
- The trend of the nineties: The careerist
- The disappearing part-time option

. . . .

Incomes—What Is Really Average?

You have read about the unlimited income potential of real estate sales. But, what does the average real estate agent make? The best figures available come from the National Association of REALTORS®, who survey their members regularly. Even though this is not a survey of all licensees (about one-half of all licensees are REALTORS®), NAR consists of the "cream of the crop"—those licensees who are willing to pay dues to contribute to the professionalism of their industry.

The median income of a REALTOR® has risen steadily from $14,700 in 1980 to $22,500 in 1990. Are these figures close to what you thought? If you base your expectations on public perception, you are about $25,000 off. According to that same NAR survey, the public thinks agents are "preoccupied with making money"—and that the average agent makes $50,000 a year! We wish! This perception is probably the reason so many people investigate real estate as an easy way to make lots of money. True, it is a great way to be in business for yourself without great financial risk, and it can be a wonderful career. But it is not a "piece of cake" to make $50,000 in real estate!

What do these "median" income figures mean? First, remember, that many REALTORS® have other sources of income. So, they may not want (or need) to earn more than this amount of money from their real estate career. Second, this is a median. It includes all new agents. As we've already discussed, it takes a while for a new agent to get established in his career. From my career selling real estate, and my management experience, I know that it takes two to three years to build a "dream career" in real estate. Why? Because, as you make more people happy by selling more real estate to them, your potential for referrals grows. It is much easier to work with someone who already thinks you are wonderful, so your business gets to be more fun and more financially rewarding. That is why it is so important for agents new to the business to start out fast, creating a pool of potential return and referral business—in order to reap those rewards in years two and beyond.

A Disturbing Trend

Although an agent's income has increased, the average number of transactions completed per agent has declined, from 16 in 1980 to 13 in 1988. The agent is earning more dollars but helping fewer people. Selling homes creates happy customers and clients that, in turn, creates the long-term goal; an expanding referral business. Because agents are selling fewer homes, the average agent is not effectively building his business. I said average, because great agents today are completing more transactions than ever before. But there are three important differences between being average and being great:

1. The agent making a significant income today sets short-term goals to make money fast and long-term goals to build an ever-increasing business.
2. The great agent's goal is to help more buyers and sellers; the dollars will be there as a result of building a business by helping lots of people buy and sell homes.
3. The great agent realizes that satisfied customers and clients create more business.

The NAR statistics show that agents are capturing more commission dollars per transaction because of increased home prices (more dollars when you sell a home), and because of graduated commission splits (companies giving the agent a greater portion of the total commission dollar). But, rather than complete more transactions to make more money, agents choose to complete fewer—and make about the same amount of money. This phenomenon increases the chasm between agents who are creating an ever-more-successful career, and those who are just "treading water."

What the Pros Make

According to the NAR study of 1990, nine percent of the agents surveyed closed over 30 transactions that year. That means, using NAR's average per transaction of approximately $1,600, 9 percent of the agents made over $50,000.

For agents who are serious about real estate as a career, an income of $50,000 after year one or two is attainable. Using the idea of *critical activities* as explained in Chapter 3, I have helped agents new to real estate make almost $100,000 their first year in the business.

One of these agents, Nada Sundermeyer, had just moved to this area. She had never been in real estate sales, but had sold hotel convention space in Cincinnati. Nada and I worked together to create a business-producing activity plan, based on the principles in Chapter 3. Nada went out and found many potential buyers; thus, she made a sale her first month in the business and completed over 35 transactions her first year. Her fourth year in the business, she made $450,000—without an assistant. Nada is a virtual whirlwind of energy and activity. She is an example of talent, enthusiasm, desire and working hard at the *right activities*.

As we investigate types of agents and incomes, I will give you other examples of agents who started their businesses and got the kind of results I regard as good—good enough to establish a really productive, professional career by year three.

You Get Back What You Put Into It

You're might ask, "Why would I want to go into business for myself if the chances are that I'll make $22,500?" We know, though, that averages really do not represent real life; for example, the 'average' American family consists of 1.5 children. Looking at an average real estate income is misleading. People enter real estate for many reasons, which are reflected in their incomes:

- Some want to make "a little extra money"—and that is what they will make.
- Some are dedicated and serious about real estate as a career so they set career goals and work hard.
- Some, unfortunately, want someplace to go so they can say they go to work. Guess how much money they make.

Three major variables determine a person's income in real estate:

1. Reasons for entering the field (earn a little extra money or career change)
2. Motivation to succeed in real estate
3. Kind and amount of activities the person is willing to do to succeed in real estate

The person's internal motivation to succeed is a much more important determinant of success than whom he or she knows, the area or the person's age or background.

The "Good Market" Theory

There is really no good or bad time to go into the market, and there are no bad markets for good real estate salespeople, unless there is a major, long-term economic catastrophe in the area. But, you have heard that there are good times to go into real estate, right? A good time is when rates are low, buyers are buying, and sellers are cooperative. Dream on! There are no perfect markets.

I learned as a sales agent that when the market is sluggish, it is a great time to enter real estate. I had been selling for six years and each year had increased my income. I had attained recognition as one of the top ten agents at my 400-agent company. Then in 1980–81 the interest rates went to 20 percent. Many agents got out of the business while I continued to make more money. Visiting another office, I ran into one of their top agents, Bob Flynn, who was consistently among the top 1 percent of all the agents in the area. We started talking about the high interest rates. I told him that, although I was doing better than ever, I was concerned about being told that this was a tough market, and "you can't make money in real estate when the interest rates are high." Bob, "Mr. Real Estate Success," who had been in real estate a decade longer than I had, assured me that good agents do better in slow markets, and that I would continue to do better. Why? Good agents work the market they are given, while poor agents sit around and complain about the market. When homes aren't selling because of high interest rates, good agents help sellers create new marketing strategies to attract serious buyers—creative financing, better pricing, better preparation of the home to show.

Poor agents just do not work in challenging markets. Instead, they sit around complaining about the state of the market or they get out of real estate. In the nineties, though, agents who come in and out of the business because they do not like the market just cannot compete with the pros—who capture and keep their customers and clients. And, consumers expect more service for their money than order taking.

How the Area Where You Work Affects Your Income

It makes sense that, the higher the home prices, the greater the sales commission. So, in market areas where there is a large, expensive inventory pool of homes, agents can potentially make a greater income than in a smaller, less expensive market area. However, there is much more competition in that kind of high-end market. The Eastside, a suburb of Seattle, Washington, is an example of that type of area where the home prices are high. It is a transferee destination where homes sell every five years and the agents are very professional and competitive.

The beauty of a smaller market is that you, the agent, can build your career on the best source of long-term business—referrals. You will not have so much competition and your cost of living is lower.

Four Categories of Salespeople

Categorized by their expectations of real estate, salespeople fall into four groups. My surveys show that there are average income ranges for each of these groups:

1. *Part-timers:* Those whose monetary goal is to make a little money in their spare time, or in retirement, or while working weekends, etc. As you might imagine, the average income for this group is a few hundred to a few thousand dollars per year.
2. *Underachievers:* Those who, during their careers, fail to produce much income because they do not find enough qualified prospects fast enough to list and sell a reasonable number of homes yearly. They may spend time at the office but not in business-producing activities. Generally, they know what to do but just refuse to do these activities consistently. The average for this group is about $7,000–15,000 per year. They get some business by waiting for prospects to come to them (an iffy way to guarantee your income).
3. *Business maintainer:* These agents have all the money they need and still sell real estate because they enjoy the work. They make enough money yearly to meet their needs (around $18,000–30,000). Many times, business maintainers have another source of income. Their strategy is to wait for business, so they expend relatively little effort actively prospecting for buyers and sellers.
4. *Careerists:* These agents look at real estate as a career. They are willing to do the sales-generating activities in the numbers required to start and perpetuate a successful real estate business. The income range for careerists in their second to third year is $25,000–40,000. I have personally hired and trained people who, in their second and third years, made $60,000–120,000. The

long-term earning potential (from approximately year three onward) for the dedicated careerist is $50,000–250,000. A few agents make $250,000–600,000, representing the top 1 percent of agents nationally. See Figures 4.1 and 4.2.

Differentiating the Careerist What exactly is a careerist? This is the person who enters real estate with the intention of creating an income comparable to that of other professional careers. The careerist prepares for real estate by taking the best postlicense practical education and training available, sets up a business plan with business-producing activities and a budget and commits one full year to establishing the business. He or she joins a group of people who have similar goals.

Careerist versus Professional It is important to differentiate the term *careerist* from the term *professional*. In the real estate industry a professional is known as a real estate agent who:

- has been working at least a few years in real estate sales;
- has attained more knowledge about real estate than he or she had as a new agent; and
- works reasonably long hours.

What is left out of this definition? Income. Using the definition above, experienced real estate salespeople call themselves professionals even if they made $1.95 from real estate sales the year before. In other words, some of those experienced agents who label themselves professional are certainly not creating incomes commensurate with professionals in other careers.

Careerists Enter Real Estate—A Nineties Trend Much greater numbers of dedicated, career-minded people are entering the real estate field. And, for those people, there is a bright income potential. In fact, the smartest real estate companies today design programs to help the careerist get started quickly, in order to swiftly replace the income enjoyed in his or her former career while creating the foundation for a very successful, lucrative real estate business.

Figure 4.1 Average Earning Potential by Type

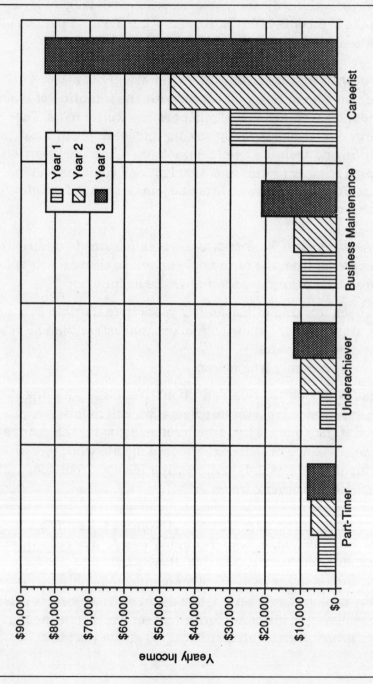

Figure 4.2 Careerists' Income Potential

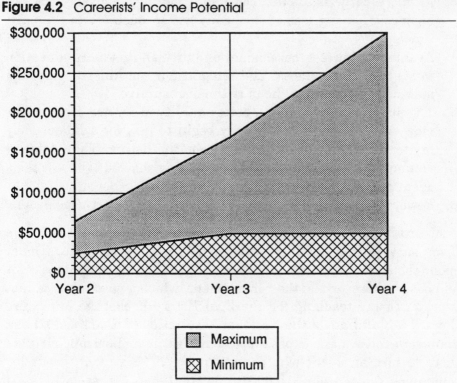

The Disappearing Part-Time Option

The Disappearing Part-Time Option

According to the National Association of REALTORS®' 1991 *Horizon* report, part-timers now account for 19 percent of all REALTORS®. Although no figures are available, I would guess that the percentages of licensees (non-REALTORS®) who are part-timers would be much higher. NAR predicts that, in the future, there will be many fewer part-timers. Why? In the nineties working in real estate sales part-time is becoming more difficult for the following reasons:

1. The start-up costs of real estate sales are higher than ever before.
2. Licensing requirements, including prelicense and postlicense education, are escalating and will continue to escalate.

3. As more careerists enter the field, they aggressively seek out business, leaving less of the easily gotten business to the part-timer.
4. Agents must invest more money and time and get more education to stay in the business. The competition continues to heat up, making it difficult for the part-timer to survive.
5. The public is demanding a better quality of service. They interview several agents before they begin to look for a home. They invite several agents to compete for the listing. They demand resumes and testimonials. They are being advised to choose their agent carefully, just as they would choose their doctor.
6. Fewer real estate companies are willing to hire part-time people.

According to the *Horizon* report, 67 percent of the most profitable firms surveyed do not hire part-timers. Because companies must spend thousands of dollars to train new agents, these companies want and deserve a return on their investment, which a part-timer cannot provide. In my teaching for the Real Estate Brokerage Managers Council (an affiliate of the National Association of REALTORS®), I ask managers and owners across the nation to estimate how much it costs them to hire an agent who doesn't "make it." Six-month costs for companies range from $15,000 to $40,000. You can see why good companies are very careful whom they hire. With that kind of investment, you would be careful, too. In addition, companies know that, to retain their customers and clients, they must keep providing a higher level of customer service through hiring and training dedicated, service-oriented careerists.

The Real-Life Challenges For a Part-Timer

Now you know why the part-time option is less attractive in today's real estate world. Now, let's look at the sales situations part-timers can find themselves in:

• You have another job but a buyer you have been working with wants to purchase a property now. He knows there has been lots of interest in the property, and is afraid, if he doesn't get his offer to purchase signed in the next two hours, he might lose the property. How will you explain to the buyer that you can't help him now because you have to go to your other job? And, could you miss earning a commission for your work when the buyer, in frustration, goes to another company?

- An offer to purchase comes in on your listing, and the seller expects you to go to the offer presentation to represent him. However, it's time to go to your other job. How do you explain that you cannot represent the seller's best interests, especially when he is paying you thousands of dollars for representation?
- How will you generate enough prospects quickly enough to earn income in your first few months in real estate while your expenses in real estate continue? As you saw in the weekly schedule for a new agent, careerists who want to replace their previous income fast and build a successful career plan on spending four hours a day finding prospects.
- How will you compete for customers and clients with a full-time, dedicated careerist?

Because of these challenges, it's becoming less and less common in the nineties to see someone work on a part-time basis over a period of years.

How about Being a Part-Timer Until I Start Making Money in Real Estate?

Frequently, a person who doesn't have sufficient savings to cover the first few months, considers keeping his or her old job while starting in real estate part-time. The agent thinks it possible to earn enough in real estate part-time to pay expenses and launch his or her career. However, it takes a great deal of effort, time, dedication and skill just to start generating sales prospects. Therefore, the person trying to hold an old job while starting a new sales career quickly becomes discouraged.

Instead of attempting to start a new sales career while holding down another job, here are some alternatives:

- Borrow sufficient capital from some source to go into real estate full-time from the beginning; you'll need a few months to get your business started and those few months require intensive, 100 percent effort. One of the most successful agents in our area told me that he borrowed on each of his charge cards so he could go into the real estate business. Was he ever compelled to succeed! I am not suggesting that you put yourself at risk to enter real estate. I am suggesting that you take actions that demonstrate your dedication to succeed.

- Work in a real estate company in a staff position to learn the business from that perspective. Then, go full-time into sales. My current secretary, at 23, is doing just that. She can be much more organized, understand all of the jargon and, from watching agents operate, know whom to emulate—and what contributes to providing high levels of customer satisfaction.

- Work at two salaried jobs to save sufficient capital to go into real estate. You will find that better than entering real estate part-time.

Summary

At the beginning of this chapter, you asked a simple question about earning potential. This certainly is not a simple answer. Here are the major points in this chapter concerning income expectations:

- Although the median income for real estate salespeople is modest, that median represents agents whose business goals differ.

- The dedicated careerist can earn an income comparable to that of other professions, an income that grows as the careerist's competence and sales record grow over a period of years.

- Social, cultural and economic trends make it increasingly difficult for a salesperson to enter part-time or to earn income that exceeds expenses.

- Real estate incomes are mainly determined by a person's motivation for entering real estate, his or her income needs from real estate sales and his or her kind and number of sales-generating activities—not the amount of time spent at the office.

5 Your Business—
Costs and Income

"You can make money in your first few months in real estate. But, the goal is to build money. Real estate is a career that gets easier and more profitable with time. Be in real estate for the long term or don't waste your time. You are definitely paying your dues at the beginning, so don't get out of the business when your dues are trying to pay you back!"

—Renee Menti, high first-year producer, former airline stewardess

In This Chapter ....

- What It costs to get started
- The tools you will need
- Ongoing costs to budget for
- For the careerist: When to expect your first check
- When you reach "breakeven"
- On the sales path to success: What to expect at the end of your first year
- Opening your own business

. . . .

What It Costs To Get Started

Jerry Turner started his real estate career with no idea that he would not receive a paycheck within one month. He had been in printing sales and management for what seemed "practically my whole life, so I knew I could sell." However, he did not know how much money was going to go out each month just to get him into the business and keep him there. "I didn't know the time frame to find a customer, show homes, sell him something, and wait to get paid. Before they go into real estate, real estate agents need to know their start-up expenses, ongoing expenses and a time frame (if they work hard) for expecting to earn their first paycheck."

So, with Jerry's advice in mind, this chapter explains agents' expenses, time frames and monetary expectations for their first year in the real estate business.

Initial Costs Are Relatively Small

When you consider that, in real estate sales, you are immediately in business for yourself, the initial costs of setting up your business are relatively small. Figure 5.1 is an itemization of typical initial costs. These are the costs you will incur before and immediately after

---

Figure 5.1   Agent Start-Up Costs

Prelicense Course:

Course	$165–$200
Test fee	$ 50

At Affiliation:

Licensing fee	$ 75	
Multiple listing key charge	$ 50	
Postlicense courses	$125–$1,200	
Business cards	$ 45	
Financial calculator	$ 40+	
Daily planner	$ 20+	
REALTOR® dues (Local, state, national)	$290+	(prorated down depending on which month you join)
Tools of the trade	$200	(briefcase, supplies, etc.)

Total: $1,000–$1,500

This list is for example only. Costs are approximate. Check with the companies in your area for their costs, the multiple listing service costs and local REALTOR® costs.

---

you are licensed. They include studying for your real estate license, affiliating with a company, activating your real estate license and beginning your career. When you interview with various companies, be sure to get—in writing—their lists of probable initial and ongoing costs.

Figure 5.2 is a sample list of the materials and services essential in real estate sales. Using this list when you interview, find out which services are provided and paid for by the company, which are shared by agent and company and which are paid for by the agent.

Normally, a list like this, in much more detail, is attached to the contract you sign at affiliation.

Figure 5.2   Essential Supplies and Services

Facilities and Equipment
  Office space
  Copy machine, fax machine
  Kroll books, MLS terminals
  Computer, printer
  Telephones, local calls
  Coffee and tea supplies

Supplies
  MLS forms
  Company stationery
  Company listing presentation

Signage
  For sale signs
  Open house signs
  Sold by signs

Brochures, Support Services
  Answering service
  Manager, support staff

Advertising
  Newspapers, magazines
  Other media

Errors and Omissions Insurance

Education

Sign Posting

Special Facilities

Agent's Personal Promotion
  Brochures
  Stamps
  Bulk mail

Beware of Additional Fees It has become common for companies to try to recapture some of the costs they have through monthly billing of small expenses to agents. For example, one company tacked on a $10 per month marketing fee. Another company attached a $25 transaction fee.

The Bottom Line on Start-Up Expenses On average, figure on spending from $500 to $1500 as you begin your career. Generally, the two largest costs are REALTOR®/multiple service affiliation and initial postlicense training program.

Materials You Need To Begin Your New Career Figure 5.3 is a list of materials that you will need for your office and your car. Total materials will be about $200–300.

Figure 5.3 Tools of the Trade

Briefcase
Pen
Pencil
Colored pen or pencil
Hi-Liter
Daily planner
Business cards
Calculator
MLS book
Street map
Tape measure (100 ft)
Reference book
Conventional loan information
FHA/VA information
Title insurance rates
Escrow insurance rates
Fire insurance rates
Calendar
Staple gun
Paper clips
Staple remover
Stick on notes

Car Trunk
Sold sign
Tape (sticky)
Mallet and nails
Screw driver
Flashlight
Coveralls
Overshoes
First–aid kit

Forms
Purchase and sale agreements
MLS change orders
Addendum forms
Listing forms

Company Materials
Special programs
Listing presentations

Your Car—Your Second Office   Typically, real estate agents drive 15,000–25,000 miles a year. Truly, their second office is their car. In fact, real estate agents say that having a comfortable, reliable car is very important to them. Because most real estate salespeople both list and sell homes, they need a large enough car to show homes to a family of four. Successful selling agents know how important it is to make customers comfortable as they look at homes. As a new real estate agent, I had a sports car, which I drove to work only when I had no appointments to show homes. But, customers would call me to ask if they could see a particular home again that afternoon. I would be stuck without the means to show them in my car. I learned the hard way that you cannot control the customer unless you have that customer in your car, getting their impressions as you drive and guiding the tour. You'd be surprised what you learn in casual conversation. At first, when buyers don't know or trust you, they are reticent about sharing their fondest dreams with you. To sell them a home, you must know their fondest dreams. As you get to know them, and, as often happens, even get lost with them as you struggle to find those properties you previewed, you and they become "human" to one another, instead of merely a salesperson and buyers. So, leave your zippy sports car or cozy two-door at home and drive your dependable, midsized sedan or passenger van.

What Kind of Car?   Remember how much money the public thinks we make? And agents' reputed overconcern with money? Be careful, when you choose your car, to give the impression that you spend your money wisely, just as you will help your customers and clients to do. Don't appear "flashy," unless you know that your best source of customers and clients will feel comfortable with a flashy agent; a few agents can get away with it. Janine was comfortably wealthy and proud of it, She wore beautiful clothes and jewelry and drove a large Mercedes. Because her clientele largely came from her social group, she was accepted. However, to a young, struggling couple attempting to buy their first home, the combination of car, clothes and jewelry was so intimidating that they asked me to refer them to a "less rich real estate salesperson who would empathize with their needs."

Adequate Insurance Coverage. Companies require certain auto insurance coverage. When you interview with your "finalist" companies, find out what auto coverage they require and check your insurance policy to be sure your coverage is adequate.

Ongoing Costs to Budget For   Figure 5.4 shows typical monthly costs that you must budget for. These include the costs of personal marketing materials and marketing a listing, selling costs, communication costs (car phone, pager), multiple listing dues, and the costs of entertainment, gifts, promotion, education and office supplies. The good news is that most of these expenses are tax-deductible, as shown in Figure 5.5. See your accountant as you begin your career, to set up a recordkeeping system for these expenses, enabling you to give your accountant accurate, correctly collated figures for tax computation. Also, the Internal Revenue Service has stringent rules on recordkeeping for business expenses. *Do not try to save money by doing your taxes yourself!*

Before entering real estate, I worked my way through college and graduate school playing piano in a band. I kept records of my expenses and filed my own tax returns. After a few years, I went to an accountant, who told me I had paid needless taxes because I had not computed my tax correctly. He also said I was lucky that I had not gotten audited because of the "creative way" I had completed my tax return.

One of the real benefits of being self-employed is the ability to write off many of your expenses to your business. Do it right from the beginning. Find an accountant who works with real estate salespeople. For the few hundred dollars you pay, you will be thousands ahead. And, you will have peace of mind. If you are audited, you know that your records are maintained to withstand IRS scrutiny. (I know. I have been audited several times).

These costs vary greatly, depending on the materials and services provided by your office, your dedication and desire to build your career fast, and your ability to dedicate resources and dollars to your best sources of business.

To get an idea of your total expenses, complete the worksheet (Figure 5.6) to figure your other normal monthly living expenses.

Figure 5.4 Approximate Monthly Costs

Multiple listing service (MLS) fees	$50
Fee for receiving all the services that the multiple listing service provides. In some areas MLS and REALTOR® services are combined.	
Errors and omissions insurance	$10
Fee for insurance against lawsuits; companies may "self-insure" or buy an insurance policy; check with the companies you interview with to find out the kind of insurance they provide—and the cost	
Promotional	$50–$200
Costs associated with marketing your listed properties: flyers, food for open houses, gifts for sellers, etc.	
Miscellaneous	$50
Costs associated with selling a home; gifts for buyers, etc.	
Communication costs	$75–$150
Car phone, long distance calls, a pager, etc.	
Entertainment, gifts	$50–$100
Promotion costs associated with getting and keeping customers	
Education	$25–$50
Continuing education, such as sales skills courses, law updates, etc.	
Office supplies	$25–$75
Personal promotion	$25–$300
Promoting yourself to get new business and to keep old business, such as personal brochures, flyers, advertising	
Other personal promotion expenses:	$200+
Personalized for sale signs	$80+
Personalized name signs for use on for sale sign	$50+
Personalized open house signs	$70+

Figure 5.5   Tax-Deductible Expenses

Make an envelope for each category. Each time you spend money for one of the following items, record the expense on a monthly receipt envelope and save the receipt in the envelope. Check with your accountant for the specifics regarding records that must be kept in each category and how they must be kept to meet IRS requirements.

Car
  Gas
  Parking fees
  Tolls
  Repairs
Dues and Fees
  REALTOR® dues
  MLS
  Designations
Entertainment
  Meals
  Rooms
  Tickets
Gifts and Gratuities
  Housewarmings
Travel for Work
  Transportation
  Lodging/Meals
  Incidentals
  Cab fare
Education
  Continuing education
  Meetings
  Conventions
  Subscriptions
  Educational tapes
  Books
Office Expenses
  Secretarial

Stationery and Supplies
  Postcards
  Mailing envelopes
  Pencils, pens, paper
  Film
  Postage
  Shipping
Marketing
  Newspaper ads
  Flyers
  Newsletters
  Brochures
Telephone
  % of service
  Long distance
  Credit card calls
  Answering service/machine/pager
Travel and Transportation
  Hotel/motel
  Taxis
  Car rental
  Meals
  Incidentals
Professional Tools
  Tape recorder
  Tape measure
  Camera
  Calculator
  Typewriter
  Adding machine
  Computer & programs

Figure 5.6   Determine Your Normal Monthly Living Expenses

House payment or rent	$_____	Property taxes and insurance	$_____
Condominium fees	$_____		
Food	$_____	Utilities	$_____
Credit cards	$_____	Incidentals	$_____
Entertainment, gifts	$_____	Clothing	$_____
Savings	$_____	School costs	$_____
Dental, medical	$_____	Health, life insurance	$_____
Car	$_____	Donations, church	$_____
(Payment, gasoline, insurance, repair)		Miscellaneous	$_____
	Total monthly costs	$_____	

Your Expenses for the First Six Months

Look at those expenses as they accrue each month to see how much you are spending during your first six months in the business. As figured earlier, each month approximately $300 to $700 goes toward business expenses. In addition, you will need your personal monthly expenses to find the total you will need each month as you start your real estate career.

How much in savings will you need? It will take you three to six months to get your first paycheck (this chapter will show you how that works). For now, here is a formula to compute your total first six months' expenses:

1. Your estimated start-up expenses: _____
2. Your estimated real estate expenses monthly × 6: _____
3. Your other monthly living expenses × 6: _____
4. Total money required (either savings or income) for your first six months in real estate: _____

Your Real Estate Income

Let's reflect back to Jerry Turner's advice at the beginning of this chapter. Yes, experienced salespeople enter real estate every day. And, yes, they begin doing the business-generating activities in great numbers on the first day of their real estate careers. And, yes, it still takes *them* a few months to get their first paycheck. Let's see why. Using that kind of career-oriented person as a model, let's track the amount of time it will take a careerist to generate a first sale, and then a first paycheck.

The Careerist's Scenario

The careerist, contacting hundreds of potential prospects the first month, finds several qualified buyers. He or she shows them homes, knowing that, on average, buyers look for homes from four to twelve weeks (according to an NAR study). Because this agent has qualified buyers, and has prioritized them according to urgency to buy, he or she sells one home at the end of the first month in the business.

Because it takes about two months to *close* a home, this careerist receives his or her first paycheck at the *end of month three.* In his or her office, the average commission to an agent is $2,000. Figure 5.7 adds time frames to the sales cycle, to show when sales-producing activities lead to commission dollars.

Breakeven From studying earning patterns and expenses of starting careerists, I've found that business expenses and income reach breakeven at about month six or seven. That means checks the agent receives by the end of this period will pay for the *business* expenses accrued from all those months. Continuing this earning pattern, the careerist will, at the end of the year, have been paid enough generally to cover all personal and business expenses—and establish an earning pattern that will propel him or her into a very successful second and third years.

Because this new agent is learning new sales skills and contacting more people while getting comfortable with the operations and information about real estate, the number of people he or she can work with at one time will increase through the months. It is uncommon,

Figure 5.7 Sales Cycle Time Frame

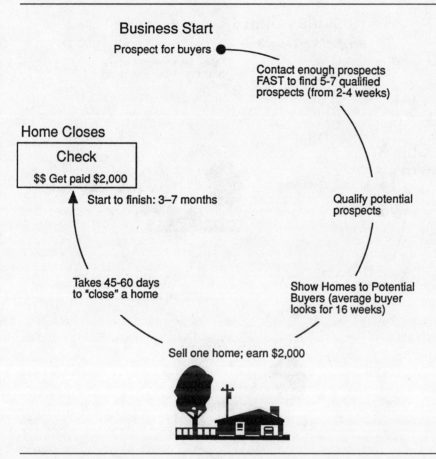

Business Start

Prospect for buyers

Contact enough prospects
FAST to find 5-7 qualified
prospects (from 2-4 weeks)

Home Closes

Check

$$ Get paid $2,000

Start to finish: 3–7 months

Qualify potential
prospects

Takes 45-60 days
to "close" a home

Show Homes to Potential
Buyers (average buyer
looks for 16 weeks)

Sell one home; earn $2,000

though, for even a dedicated careerist to generate enough prospects
to sell more than one home the first month or two in the business. In
addition to the sale, the careerist finds several prospects who are
interested in selling their properties. So, in the second month in the
business, the careerist lists a property at a marketable price—a
property that will sell within a reasonable time frame, which, in the
careerist's area, is 90 days. Fortunately, that listed property does sell
in 90 days. The home closes in two months. Now it is seven months
into the agent's career. Again, the commission to the agent is $2,000.

Figure 5.8   Listing Cycle Time Frame

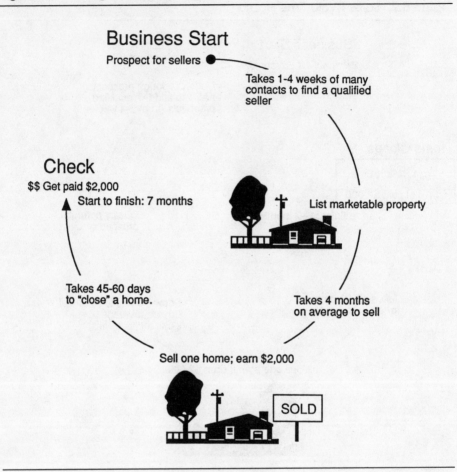

Business Start
Prospect for sellers ●

Takes 1-4 weeks of many
contacts to find a qualified
seller

Check
$$ Get paid $2,000
Start to finish: 7 months

List marketable property

Takes 45-60 days
to "close" a home.

Takes 4 months
on average to sell

Sell one home; earn $2,000

SOLD

Look at Figure 5.8, where time frames are attached to the listing version of the sales cycle. From the time frames involved in selling and listing real estate, you can see why new agents are advised to *sell homes* for the fastest income.

Early Dumb Luck   Yes, you say, but you have heard about agents selling a home at an open house their first month in the business. I call that dumb luck. Still, let's use that scenario to plan when you would get your first check. You meet a buyer during your first week in the business. This buyer wants to buy that home and can close the transaction in 45 days. You write the offer to purchase and it is accepted. The transaction closes in 45 days. You receive your check in your second month in the business.

Let's get serious. How many times does that actually happen? In nine years of real estate sales, I have seen very few agents meet and close a buyer in their first week of real estate.

A Set-Up for Failure   I found in my study that the largest group of new agents expected to receive a check by their *third month* in the business. They believed that, armed with a real estate license, lots of information, and business cards, they were qualified to sell a home—and that they would easily find someone and sell them a home—fast. But, even more alarming was the information they gave me that they could *only* stay in the business *four* months without a paycheck. If managers knew new agents' expectations for early success—and the *need* for a paycheck in those first few months, they would manage new agents differently. Instead of leaving new agents to their own devices, or at most, chatting with them weekly, managers would closely manage new agents with an effective business-producing activity plan. (See Appendix C for available plans.)

The Careerist's Income at the End of the First Year

The careerist's first goal as he goes into real estate is to generate hundreds of qualified prospects. He or she realizes that some of these prospects will not be buyers or sellers for months—or years. This results in selling more properties consistently as the months go by. He or she lists more and more properties, which begin to sell. In other words, in the first year, the careerist generates an increasing number of transactions. By the end of the first year, the careerist has built a solid foundation for a great career. Typically, following the careerist pattern, an agent makes $25,000 to $40,000 the first year in real estate. Look at the time line (Figure 5.9) to see how this career grows at the end of the first year.

Figure 5.9 Careerist Timeline

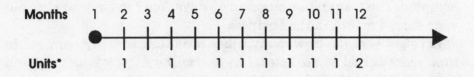

*A unit is a sale or a listing sold and is worth $1,000–$2,500 for a new agent. So, in this scenario, the careerist has established a solid foundation for a career by closing ten transactions the first year in real estate.

What Is "Enough"?

Each month, I teach a business planning course to new agents. I ask them how many transactions in an agent's first year would be adequate to build a career. At first, they usually estimate 24! From that, I know they have no idea how many transactions the average REALTOR® completes (the NAR survey indicated for all REALTORS® it was 13). Then, I ask them for minimum expectations to build a career. They settle on twelve. I think that is a good number, because it is enough

- to create sources of referral business
- to keep the new agent's self-esteem high—and keep him going through the rough spots
- to help him get really *good* at selling real estate

Figure 5.10 shows how happy buyers and sellers multiply your chances of building a powerful business in years two and three if you stay in contact with them. Marketing advice to careerists: Treat the old customer like the appreciating asset he or she is. This is a trend of the nineties. Smart agents are creating marketing plans directed at old customers and clients, so they can reap more business from their *best* sources—those sellers and buyers who already think the agent is wonderful! (The business planning system in Appendix C gives detailed information about this strategy.)

Figure 5.10 How Buyers Multiply

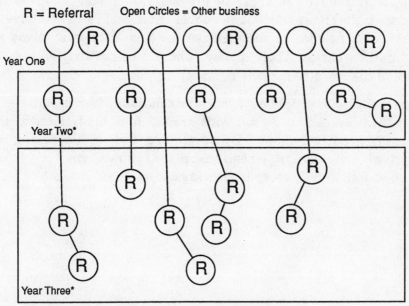

R = Referral   Open Circles = Other business

Year One

Year Two*

Year Three*

* Plus sales and listings from sources other than referrals

Happy customers, contacted frequently, "beget" referrals, which grow yearly.

You can reap big rewards year three in real estate.

Summary

This chapter itemizes the start-up and ongoing costs related to real estate sales. Important principles in this chapter are:

- Initial costs vary greatly with area and company.
- Ongoing costs vary greatly by company and are related to the company's commission splits.
- Even though the careerist does the kind and amount of activities that generate income early in his or her career, there are still certain time frames associated with the buyers' decision-making process, the property time on market and closing. These time

frames result in a commission for the new agent, at the earliest, in
month three or four of his career.

- It is very important that the new agent plan to have four to six
  months' income in savings, to provide the chance to generate
  business. Unfortunately, many people enter real estate to "give it
  a try," with no idea of the expenses or time frames involved in
  beginning a career. Their money runs out before they can enjoy
  reaping the rewards of their prospecting work.

Even though you should have four to six months of savings to begin
your real estate career, do not wait around four to six months for
"something good to happen." By developing and implementing an
aggressive business plan, you can ensure that you will get a paycheck
early, to be followed by an ever-growing career.

6 How To Become Licensed

> *"Get your prelicense training from a reputable real estate training school. Don't think, though, that the course fully prepares you to sell real estate. The prelicense training does not prepare you adequately for face-to-face contact with customers and clients—a skill that is essential to success."*
>
> —Connie Walsh, top 10% of her company, former chef

In This Chapter . . . .

- Requirements for becoming licensed
- Prelicense courses and schools
- Informational resources
- Time frames for becoming licensed
- Tips for passing the test
- What passing the test means
- Other courses you'll need

. . . .

So far, you are still in the game. You love the thought of being independent, and you are excited about the challenge and responsibility of creating your own business—and your own income. Here are the steps you will take to get a license.

Requirements for Becoming Licensed

Agencies Responsible for Licensing Regulations

Each of the 50 states and each of the provinces of Canada has some type of governmental agency responsible for the administration of the real estate license laws. This agency makes rules regarding real estate practice, enforces laws governing real estate licensees and sets criteria, including educational standards, for prelicensing and postlicensing requirements. The real estate licensing agencies' duty is to protect the public interest. These agencies are all a part of the National Association of Real Estate Law Officials (NARELLO), a federation of law officials created to assist each other in the administration and enforcement of license laws in the United States and Canada. Since NARELLO's inception in 1930, a major accomplishment has been to develop uniform legislation to better protect the consuming public.

Some states incorporate into these agencies education directors, education advisory committees and an education research center or fund. The trend in the nineties is toward increasing prelicense and postlicense requirements, funds and centers, generally paid for by licensing fees.

The requirements to get your real estate license:

1. Must meet minimum age requirements (18 in most states).
2. Must pay an exam/licensing fee, which ranges from $18 to $75, depending on the state (license good for 1 to 4 years, depending on the state).
3. Must take and pass a licensing exam.

Educational Requirements   Over three-fourths of the states require the completion of certain real estate courses. These range from "home study" to 90 hours of completed class time. In some states, applicants must show proof of completing specific, prescribed courses before taking the exam. These courses prepare applicants to take and pass the exam. In addition, some states waive part or all of the educational requirements if the applicant has equivalent experience such as a real estate license in another state, or a law degree.

Information about State Requirements Appendix B lists the name, address and telephone number of the regulatory agency in your jurisdiction. The licensing fees, term of the license and prelicensing and postlicensing educational requirements of each state and Canadian province are available in a publication from NARELLO, titled *Digest of Real Estate License Laws, United States and Canada.* Published yearly, digests can be ordered for $30 by sending a check to NARELLO, P. O. Box 129, Centerville, UT 84014–0129.

Questions To Ask Your Licensing Agency Your state licensing agency will provide you with the information you need regarding the specific requirements in your state. Here are the points to cover with them:

1. Age requirement
2. Prelicense educational hours required—how many, within what time period
3. Which schools teach the courses
4. Cost of license fee—and the term of the license
5. Study materials available—and where to purchase
6. How to apply for exam
7. Where/when are exams given
8. Re-exam available—how to apply/cost
9. How to apply for license
10. Other licensing requirements—waivers

How To Study for the Exam A few states do not require the completion of clocked course hours prior to taking the test for a licensing exam. However, for most people with rusty study habits and conflicting commitments taking a course to prepare you to pass the exam, whether your state requires it or not, is highly recommended. Once you see the subject material, which is mainly memorization of facts, rules and laws, you will find it difficult to motivate yourself to study without some class accountability.

Exam Study Guides Some states publish a study guide, usually in conjunction with their testing service. When you call the regulatory agency, be sure to ask if a study guide is available. In addition, there are books available to help you study for your exam. Some of the best are listed in Appendix C. The Real Estate Education Company, an imprint of Dearborn Financial Publishing, offers books to help you pass the test that are specific to particular states. Other Real Estate Education titles are listed in Appendix C.

What Kind of School Should I Attend?

College Courses

With the constant escalation of prelicense educational requirements, all kinds of schools have leaped into the real estate education business. State and community colleges have courses to prepare you to pass the exam. Of all the courses available, these courses generally have the longest time frame, extending throughout the term or semester. If you like plenty of reflection time and class time, a state or community college is probably a good choice. Usually these courses are of good quality and are taught by knowledgeable instructors.

Private Real Estate School

As states continue to increase the educational prelicense requirements, more privately owned schools have sprung up to fill the need. Sometimes affiliated with real estate companies, they are called *proprietary schools*. Many of these schools exist just to provide prelicensing courses.

For a full listing of these schools, look in your phone book under "Real Estate Schools." Your state's regulatory agency can be helpful, too, in guiding you toward a school in your area. In addition, call a real estate company and ask to speak to a newly licensed agent. Inquire about the school he attended, and you will get a good idea of the pros and cons of each school and type of program. Real estate managers in the area where you live or work also can help you choose an appropriate prelicense program.

Questions To Ask the School   To be an accredited real estate school, the school and its administrator have to meet certain requirements of the state regulatory agency. Generally, those requirements are minimal. As you can imagine, then, schools range from excellent to mediocre. Be sure to check out the school before paying your money. Call or visit the school and find out what type of course delivery they offer; the length of the program; who teaches; who the school is affiliated with; their test "pass" rates, if available (in some states, schools aren't allowed to publish or publicize these); see the course curriculum and materials; find out what the fee includes; and ask if there is an additional fee for a "cram" course prior to the exam. Finally, get recommendations from their students. Choose the study program that best fits your needs.

Type of Study Programs

Live Lecture   Usually takes 6 to 13 weeks to complete; is in lecture format, with one or more "live" instructors. Group discussion can be interesting, but can get you off track, for there are all types of people in the "live" class, including those studying for their brokers' exams. If you are the kind of person who likes to learn with others, this format is for you. Lecture format is used in college programs and some private proprietary schools. In addition, some private schools offer classroom format in "cram" courses. You will get lots of information verbally but must study on your own to assimilate and memorize it.

Visual Slide Presentation with Audio Support   This is a self-study program you can take at your own speed. It consists of slides, workbooks, and sample tests. If you like studying on your own, and learn visually, you will enjoy this type of course.

Computer Programs   There are some new interactive computer programs that consist of software, workbooks and sample tests. If you like working on your own, you may want to investigate this type of program.

Audio Study Program   This program is audio only; you listen to audio tapes and complete workbook assignments. You can study at your own speed. Sample tests are included. If you like to learn by listening, choose this type of program. It is very helpful in preparing for the kind of multiple-choice testing that the licensing exams use. The information can be updated quickly, so learners get the advantage of law changes, testing changes, etc. My husband, a radio disc jockey for 20 years, found that listening to the definitions and explanations of the concepts tested on the licensing exam helped him prepare for and pass the prelicense exam. Personally, I think that my mind would wander too much listening to that material on audiotape! Each of us needs to assess our favorite learning style, time frame and budget when choosing a program.

The Real Estate Exam

All 50 states and the Canadian provinces require an exam prior to licensing. These exams are given regularly throughout the year in various testing sites within each state and province. Generally, the licensee's exam is about four hours in length. Each state's test is divided into two areas:

1. National material—covering areas common to all states (financing, contracts, brokerage, valuation and ownership)
2. State material—covering areas specific to that state (rules, regulations, laws, procedures)

The Nature of the Test Questions There are approximately 100 questions on a licensing exam. All of the test questions are multiple choice; they ask the applicant to recall definitions, laws and licensing rules and to compute simple real estate math problems. In most states, "passing" is 70 to 75 percent. Some states combine the scores of both sections of the exam. In others, applicants must pass each section but may take only one section again if they fail a particular section.

Math About 20 to 25 percent of the questions on the exam will require mathematical computations. This fact strikes fear in the hearts of many readers, right? Not to worry. This math is basic arithmetic, about the level you studied in the 6th to 8th grades. However, if you feel shaky about this area (and it is common to feel that way), take a business math, basic math, or math review course at your community college. The Real Estate Education Company also has two mathematics books, listed in Appendix C, to improve your skills in real estate math. The good news is that this sharpening of your skills will pay off when you start selling real estate, because you will be putting the math skills you learned to work. In fact, you will probably find that the math skills you review in your prelicense course will be the most practical material you will later use in your career.

Studying Tips The exam is a means to control the number of applicants into a field. The exam questions deal with some pretty esoteric material. In fact, even seasoned real estate agents admit that they would have to take a course again to pass the test because they do not use that information in everyday real estate! To help you use your class and study time effectively to memorize the important information, here are some study tips:

1. Prior to each in-class session, skim the next chapter for highlights. Then, read the chapter carefully.
2. Right after class, review class subjects and notes.
3. Make a notebook with all the definitions you covered in each class session. Create test questions to match words and definitions.
4. If you learn through listening, and you are not in an audio program, audiotape yourself saying the definitions. Play these as you drive your car.
5. Keep up with the class work. Attend every session and be sure to study *regularly* between sessions.
6. Take every practice exam until you are very comfortable with the process and format.

Taking the Test Exam anxiety: we have all had it at some time. Here are a few pointers that will help you relax, control your emotions, and pass the test the first time you take it:

1. Read each question slowly; then, read all the possible answers. *Do not jump to conclusions to mark the right answer.* Instead, tell yourself *why* each answer is *wrong.* By the process of elimination,

find the only answer you think is correct. If you find two out of four that may be correct, leave that question and come back to it.
2. Do not answer any questions that you are not very sure of. Leave them and come back to them.
3. Take your time. You will have plenty of time to answer each question on the exam.
4. Build your self-confidence as you start by skimming the exam. Find some questions you are very sure of and answer them first. Amazingly, when your mind gets "warmed up," you will find you can think through questions that baffled you when you tried to attack them at the beginning of the testing period.
5. Let the test "give you the answers." By reading through the complete test first, answering only the questions you are sure of, you will find hints of other answers. Your confidence will soar, and you will find you are answering more questions as the test period goes on.

What If You Don't Pass the First Time? All states allow you to pay a re-examination fee, and take all or part of the exam again. Some states have no limit on the number of times you can retake the exam; other states have limits of three to twelve times. In states that divide the test into two sections, you'll probably be able to retake only the part of the exam you failed.

General Passing Rates Ratios of students passing the exam rage widely from state to state. For example, Maine has a 48 percent pass rate, while Oregon has an 89 percent pass rate. No matter what the rate, the important consideration for you is that it always builds more confidence to pass *any* exam the first time. So study!

What Passing the Exam Means As you can tell from the description of the exam, the content and format test how well the applicant memorized facts, rules and laws. In other words, it tests the applicant's level of *knowledge*. So, what passing the test means is that the applicant answered multiple-choice questions correctly, which proves he has accumulated lists of facts, rules and laws in his mind—at least for the short term. Remember, this exam principally serves as a screening device for regulatory agencies, to control the number of new licensees who enter the field each year.

Doesn't Passing the Test Predict Success in Real Estate? No. Connie Walsh said it well at the beginning of this chapter. Success (making money) in real estate depends on what you *do,* not what you *know.* From an earlier chapter, you know these activities are:

1. going out of the office to meet large numbers of people you can qualify as good potential customers and sellers,
2. working with qualified sellers to sell their properties,
3. working with qualified buyers to find them a property to purchase and
4. closing buyers and listing sells.

As you can tell from the prior description of what the licensing exam covers, none of these activities is tested in licensing exams. Instead, regulatory agencies leave the licensee's subsequent development of his or her business up to the broker. Why? Regulatory agencies are first concerned with "protecting the public interest." The premise of the license testing is that if licensees understand the rules and regulations regarding real estate licensees, they will, in their real estate practice, protect their customers and clients. In addition, the material tested (laws, rules and regulations) can be taught in a lecture format and tested via multiple choice. It is easy for the regulatory agency to evaluate.

The Broker's Perspective Brokers can get frustrated with the prelicense requirements and the perception they generate in new licensees that passing a multiple-choice exam means one will succeed in real estate sales. In some states, brokers, trainers and schools are working with their regulatory agencies to expand and/or to change the course curriculum, teaching methods and methods of prelicense testing to better prepare the licensee for the business. One of the considerations is to require more prelicense clock hours in the *practical* aspects of selling real estate.

Smart brokers are not waiting for prelicense standards to change. To adequately prepare their "new hires" to succeed quickly in the business world of real estate sales, companies are creating special postlicense training programs. More about what these programs are and how to find them in a later chapter.

How To Get Other Information You Need

In addition to your prelicense course requirements, you can get a taste of what real estate sales is in the "real world" by enrolling in courses that teach sales skills. One of the best is the Dale Carnegie Sales Course, taught in most larger cities. In this course, you will actually experience the tasks you will perform each day to develop your real estate business. You can find Dale Carnegie courses in the phone book. For other sales training courses, look in the yellow pages under "Sales Training." Call several companies. To find a good sales skills training course, be sure that the course is taught as "skill development." Skill development consists of learning a concept, applying it as a skill and going out to practice the skill in the "real world." Think of developing sales skills just like developing the skill to drive a car. First, you watch the instructor drive the car. Then, you drive the car with the instructor there. Finally, you drive the car alone—"in the field" (well, we hope, not really in the field). Just like learning to drive a car, sales skill is learned and perfected by doing. So, to learn these skills well from the start, you need to experience the "doing" with the instructor—and then on your own.

Besides taking a sales skills course, find out more about the business of real estate by reading books about real estate practice. Several are listed for your reference in Appendix C. In addition, take a course in "Real Estate Principles and Practices" (or similar name) at your local community college. Look at the description of the course to be sure that the course is not merely a licensing exam preparation course. In a good "practices" course, you will learn about real estate as a business; the language of the business; tips on how to make money in real estate; and how to provide high levels of customer service. In addition, you'll hear "war stories" (real estate life experiences) from participants, many of whom have already been in real estate.

Career Nights

In order to attract new agents to their company, some companies present seminars, commonly called *career nights*. When you attend such a function, you will hear about real estate as a career, how to get started, licensing requirements, etc. Because these events are held to find prospective agents, be aware that the picture painted about real estate sales could be excessively rosy. Remember, these are skilled salespeople up in front of you, presenting all the benefits of real estate sales as a high-income career. It is fine to attend such functions. Just keep in the back of your mind the reason for the career night. Judge the credibility of the presentation by the number of facts presented rather than on the motivational value of the presentation.

How Long Does It Take to Get Started?

If your state requires the completion of a course to prepare you to take the exam, much of your time frame is set by the particular course you choose. As mentioned earlier, the term or semester program at a college will be the longest format. The self-directed programs will be relatively the shortest. Check the laws of your state, and the availability of various course formats.

On average, plan on at least four weeks of study to prepare for your licensing exam. Be sure to check the application procedures in your state. Generally, states require that you apply to take the exam several weeks before an exam date. In Washington state, for example, applicants must apply to take the exam four weeks prior to the desired exam date. However, applicants may, for a larger fee, walk in and take the exam on the exam day if space is available.

Figure 6.1 provides a time line, so you can see approximate time frames, from the time you start your research to the field to the time you affiliate with a company.

When Will I Get My Exam Results?   You will receive notice that you have passed your exam within about two weeks after your exam date. With those results in hand, you may affiliate with a broker, send your application to the state (with your broker's signature) and be eligible to sell real estate. So, you will want to plan a time frame of at least

---

Figure 6.1   Time Line—From Interest to Affiliation

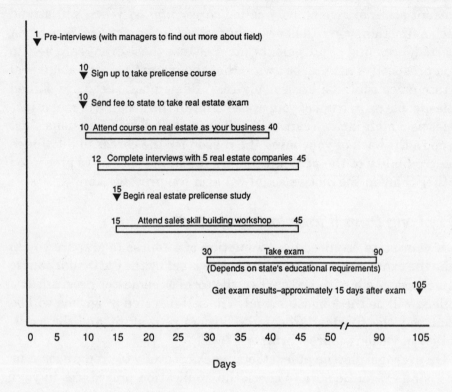

six weeks from the time you begin studying for your exam to the time you are licensed—and that's a minimum time frame. And, you will want to plan for enough savings to cover your expenses until you receive your first check.

Other Licensing Requirements

Over two-thirds of the states now require *continuing education* (CE) requirements to maintain a real estate sales license. These requirements range from 3 hours every year to 30 hours every two years. Generally, the subjects approved for license renewal are technical in nature:

- Law updates
- Finance
- Environmental issues

Some states spell out particular courses required and even include curriculum. Some states require an ethics course. Through requiring licensees to learn the facts regarding these topics, regulatory agencies can fulfill their charge to "protect the public interest." Because of the increasing number of laws, rules and regulations, keeping licensees up to date through continuing education is a large concern of regulatory agencies today.

NARELLO's "white paper" for 1992 (in NARELLO's 1992 annual report) consists of a survey regarding states' present educational requirements, challenges these states perceive they face, and recommendations they are considering for enhancing their postlicense requirements. For your state's requirements, see the NARELLO report or contact your state's regulatory agency. The managers you interview with can also tell you the continuing licensing requirements in your area.

Beyond Licensing Requirements

Knowing the updates on the laws, rules, and regulations are not enough to keep you ahead of the game as you progress in your real estate career. In addition to your knowledge of the latest in the technical facts, to become—and stay—a real careerist, you must consistently take part in skill-building sales workshops, business planning sessions, and courses that increase your ability to create a competitive business.

Excellent courses for licensed salespeople are offered through the National Association of REALTORS®. The Graduate REALTORS® Institute (GRI) is a series of courses created by NAR to help agents learn the practical and technical aspects of real estate sales. These courses are provided by state REALTOR® associations. The completion of this series results in earning the GRI designation. Call your state REALTOR® association to learn more about these courses in your area.

In addition, there are advanced courses offered by the Institutes of the National Association of REALTORS®. For salespeople, the Certified Residential Specialist (CRS®) courses, offered throughout the nation, are excellent. The completion of these courses leads to the CRS® designation. The Residential Sales Council, headquartered in Chicago, creates and administers these courses.

Your state association can also give you information about these courses offered in your area. State and some local REALTOR® associations, as a member benefit, offer excellent advanced courses for agents and managers. Again, your association can help you find courses in your area. Many companies, too, have begun to offer advanced courses to help their seasoned associates adjust to the changes in real estate practice.

Ask the Manager How a company regards continuing education—especially the practical, business-producing aspects, is important to your development as a successful agent. As you interview with managers, ask them about their continuing education programs, both in their offices and in their companies. Find out their basic philosophy regarding continuing education. One real estate company owner in our market area recently told an interviewee, "We don't believe in education. We just go out and sell real estate." It is certainly true that, to be successful, you have to "go out and do it." But, in this day in age, that is not enough. Increasing your knowledge and skill through continuing education and training is a key to high productivity and a successful, long-term real estate career in the nineties. (It is also the key to avoiding lawsuits.)

Summary

This chapter discusses licensing requirements, study tips and ongoing education. Important ideas are:

- Passing the prelicense exam does not fully prepare you to sell real estate nor is it a predictor of your success in real estate.

- The prelicense curriculum and test format may mislead agents to assume that success in real estate sales is directly related to the accumulation of facts, definitions and laws regarding real estate.
- It is important for the prospective agent to get information about selling real estate from sources other than a prelicense course. These sources include educational courses, skill-developing workshops and books about selling real estate.

7 Your Search for the Right Real Estate Office

"Selecting your real estate company has to be more like a marriage than anything. You'll want to surround yourself with people you like, an atmosphere that's comfortable, and a pace that's challenging to you. I love the little time I spend at my office."

—Liz Talley, first-year top-producing agent and former trainer for an attorney's office

In This Chapter . . . .

- Choices: Companies in the nineties
- How to assess companies in your area
- The most important considerations for you
- How to gather information from other sources
. . . .

When To Start Your Search

You are serious about a career in real estate. You have done some investigation of prelicense programs and worked on the time frames involved in studying for and taking your prelicense test. You may have already talked to some real estate companies in your area. Your next step is to gather more information about companies and offices in your area. Ideally, you will want to do this while you are studying for your licensing exam. Then, as you near your test date, begin your interviews with specific offices and managers. That way, by the time you have your exam results in hand, you will have completed most of the process of choosing the right company, office and manager for you. If, however, you have already taken and passed your real estate exam, start investigating companies and offices right away. And, take your time in making your decision. It is the most important one you will make regarding your real estate career.

Company Choices—The Trends of the Nineties

Years ago, prospective agents merely walked down the street to their well-known, independent local broker-owner, chatted a while, and "hired on." The new agent understood that the image of the company was created and perpetuated by that broker-owner. By affiliating with that owner, the new agent was assured of getting the business approach—the image—that was personified in the broker-owner. Also the agent was assured of being mentored by that broker-owner. Today, there are fewer independent, local broker-owners and many more *affiliated* offices. These affiliations may be all kinds of networks—inter-city referral companies, third-party relocation management companies, franchise organizations and even mortgage market information networks. According to NAR's Horizon report of 1991, about 35 percent of all real estate companies have some *network affiliations*. Furthermore, *three-fourths* of all salespeople licensed are in a firm with some type of network affiliation. So, in today's real estate world, the interviewee must determine not only the benefits of the manager and office, but those of any affiliations.

This chapter, will help you understand the *affiliation trends* of the nineties, and what it means to you as you interview with various offices.

The Battle of the Affiliations

Thirty years ago, all real estate companies were independent, with no local, regional or national affiliations. Generally, a new real estate company sprang up when a good salesperson got tired of working for someone else and said, "I should start my own shop. I'm a good salesperson, and I might as well keep the whole commission." Real estate companies were generally "mom and pop shops," run by good sales people—who were not necessarily good *business* people.

The Franchise Idea Meets Real Estate   As franchising became popular in many businesses in the seventies, it was inevitable that this idea would be translated to real estate. What a wonderful idea—to capture and control all those small, independent real estate businesses—to imbue the consistency of a McDonald's into these mom-and-pop real estate companies! And, early franchisees saw benefits: They could get the business services they needed to compete in an increasingly sophisticated marketplace, and they could unite in a single identity nationally for vastly increased market recognition and advertising power.

Challenges to National Franchises   As these franchises gained momentum, many real estate practitioners in the seventies predicted that this franchise idea of affiliating independent owners under one banner would rule the real estate world in the future. The eighties and nineties have shown that has not been exactly the case. One challenges to these early franchisers came from the fact that they affiliated sometimes wildly disparate owners under one set of colors. It did not work perfectly. It was like taking a neighborhood hamburger joint, putting a golden arches sign out front and thinking you now had a McDonald's!

Franchisers based in a city thousands of miles from their franchisees found it difficult to control the image they wanted to project, especially on a national level. Brokers, being salespeople with independent souls, wanted the services that the franchiser provided, but they wanted to continue to do things their way, even when it clashed with the franchiser image. So, this clash of images created confusion with the public. Also, brokers found that, to compete in their marketplaces, they had to become better business people—even with franchise benefits.

Independent Firms' Growth from Citywide to Regional   At the same time that various franchises on a national level were attempting to attract the small independent broker, another trend was developing. The large independent company, dominant in its city, grew into the market region surrounding it. This type of company understood the nuances of the area, had a dominant market share and, because it had one leader or president, marketed a consistent image within its area of expertise. So, voila! Another huge player grew to dominate market share, especially in large metropolitan areas: the regional independent company.

In the past few years, the regional independent company has increased its presence in its market area by franchising to markets close by. As you could predict from the experience of the national franchisers, some regional independents are experiencing the same image conflict. Well-prepared firms avoid these conflicts by choosing franchisees carefully, orienting new franchisees thoroughly on the image and philosophy of the company and providing strong training programs for managers and owners.

The Large National Company Seeing the potential to harness huge sources of revenue, the financial management community decided to leap into the breach, to capture disparate real estate companies under one umbrella. However, they did it differently. To avoid the challenges that confronted the franchisers, a financial management business decided to buy local independent real estate companies to create one huge national company. Then it could control the image, both in communities and on a national level. Now, this national company has added franchisees, independent local real estate companies who keep ownership but contract for the sales and management services this national entity provides. In the past few years, other financial management companies have entered the real estate business this way.

Today's Affiliates Today the affiliated category has three general arrangements:

1. Franchises that own no real estate companies but provide services to independent companies
2. Regional independent companies who also franchise
3. National companies who also franchise

In 1991, according to the NAR Horizon report, 18 percent of the real estate firms in the United States had some kind of franchise affiliation, while 32 percent of all salespeople belonged to firms with these affiliations. In addition, though, according to a survey and newsletter service, RealTrends, the market share (total business done by real estate companies) of those firms is estimated at 33 percent (study from 1989).

As you start your job search, compare the local franchises in your market area. Visit their offices. Through observation, ask yourself, "Do they convey the same image? Are their offices consistent in quality? What about their agents? Are they identifiable as a group?" The more consistency, the more you benefit, since you'll want to be a part of a unified team. The next chapter we will give you some questions to ask the manager of a particular office, so you can determine how well the company image and services are communicated to and used by the agents.

Not All Companies Are Affiliated with a Larger Entity

Some companies across the United States have chosen to remain independent. Some of the best companies around are those who have learned to compete with the giants. There is one word that describes every company that has held its own in the real estate marketing wars of the nineties: specialists. That means that a particular company has figured out what it is really good at, and has specialized in that particular product or service. In order to focus their resources and image in the marketplace, they have given up trying to be all things to all people. They do not try to do a "little of this and a little of that." Instead, they have developed sales and training programs to serve particular markets. Specialty areas in products include:

1. Builder/developer marketing and sales
2. Condominium sales
3. Resale homes in certain areas and price ranges
4. Waterfront properties
5. Land and lot sales

Specialty markets in consumer groups served include:

1. First-time buyers
2. Move–up buyers
3. Transferred buyers and sellers
4. Retirees

To compete with large independents and franchisees, the managers of these companies have had to get really good at certain skills: recruiting, selling, marketing and promotion or perhaps training. For the new agent, there are many benefits of affiliating with a manager who has personally developed the marketing and sales skills for success in the nineties.

What about a Small Town That Has No Specialists?

As I teach courses around the nation to managers and agents, real estate practitioners from smaller market areas try to tell me that they aren't specialists because their town is too small for them to specialize in certain products. However, after I chat with those who are successful salespeople and managers, I discover, that, although they do not specialize in one product only, they have built their business by becoming really good at something—either a group of products or services. For instance, one broker built his business by targeting repeat business. To get repeat business, he built customer satisfaction programs to ensure that his customers would be so happy, they would always want to work with his agents again. In addition, he trained his agents to keep in close contact with old customers and clients. He created past customer follow-up programs in his office to support his agents' activities. He built his advertising campaigns to re-attract old customers. Quite a specialist, I'd say!

Remember, specialties can be in services as well as products. So, as you consider the independent company in your area, you will want to determine what the firm's specialty is, how good they are at it and whether these specialties are the ones you want to build your business around. Chapter 8 discusses exploring those areas.

Which Is Better for Me, an Affiliate or Nonaffiliate

Each type of company organization has benefits for you. Each type also has drawbacks. Large companies with regional or national affiliations have training programs and marketing services that may not be available in small companies. Affiliated or large companies have name recognition in wider market areas, so that the agent new to the business has the benefit of attaching his name to a recognizable company in the area.

On the debit side: Sometimes a new agent can get lost in a large office. So, before you leap to an affiliated company, ask, "What does this affiliation mean to me? How will I use the services available to me? Who will personally invest his energies daily (if needed) to ensure that I get started fast?"

What Size Office Is Best for Me?

The trend is toward offices with more salespeople, because it costs less per agent to operate a large office than a small one. And, because real estate brokers are making less of a profit each year (because of operating costs and generous commission splits to agents) brokers are challenged to find a combination of agent services and reasonable profitability. Although half of the firms in the United States have five or fewer salespeople, over half the total salespeople are in three percent of the firms!

The regionalization of offices has caused this trend. *Regionalization* means that 40 to 100 agents work out of one office, to cover one market region. Even though the trend is toward larger, regionalized offices, a recent study by NAR showed that average productivity per agent was higher in a smaller office. Why? Because larger offices hire more new agents, and provide new agent training. Since it takes awhile for new agents to be productive, and some of them get out of the business quickly, the new agents pull down the average productivity per agent of large offices.

Who Is Absolutely Dedicated to Your Success?

Your concern, whether the office is large or small, is who is charged with ensuring your success. In a large office of more than 35 to 40 salespeople, you'll need to have a mentor to help you get started fast. This mentor needs to be formally trained to help new agents, have a proven new agent business-producing plan and have a systematic method to meet and counsel with you. It is not impossible, but very unlikely, that the manager of a larger office has the time, singular interest and/or expertise to devote to you the first few weeks and months you are in the business.

As the manager of a 45-person office, even with the desire, I literally did not have time to guide new agents to start their careers right—and earn money fast. So, I created a *mentor program* and ran it in my office. Some managers think that having a mentor program means you never have to speak with new agents. It is just the opposite. Mentors form another "layer" that managers need to manage. The greatest benefit of these programs is that more people in an office are dedicated to the new agent's success. Those experienced agent mentors do not want their new agents to fail, and they take any steps they need to take to ensure that new agent's success.

An agent hired two months before I became manager was sitting around, waiting for something good to happen to him. I trained a mentor for him who literally "dogged his tracks" so he would not fail. She called him every morning. She called him every night. She took him with her into the field to knock on doors and ask for business. After a month of this, the agent's business took off. Now, after three months of hard work it is paying off. He has listed four properties, sold three properties and one of his listings has sold. Now, he has got a new problem: too much business. He is tired but happy! Even if I had the time, I couldn't have done effectively what his mentor did for him.

Your Most Important Choice

You get the message. None of the company advantages means much unless you affiliate with an office and manager who represent the company in a way that is consistent with its overall image. Rather than run yourself ragged comparing company advantages, spend much more time evaluating particular offices and managers. Even in the most tightly-run real estate company, each office has its own persona, specialties and methods of operation. And, most of the persona comes from the manager. The next chapter will give you questions that reveal the ability of the manager to help you build your business—fast.

Research Companies and Offices in Your Area

If you are now studying for your license, start narrowing your search for an appropriate real estate office. By the time you are ready to take your test, you should have targeted five or six offices where you want an interview. Here are the steps to take to find those offices.

Choose Your Market Area

To be successful in today's marketing world you will need to define a specific geographic market area where you want to work. Because building your career depends on getting known in an area as a real estate expert, you will want to confine your business to an area small enough for you to develop name recognition. Here are the easiest market areas for a new agent to start:

- Where you already have friends and business acquaintances
- Where you live, because you know the area and its businesses and service people

Friends and Business Contacts Agents in the business one to two years did not initially find their friends to be their best source of business. That is because friends, who know you in a different way, are waiting to see if you make it in real estate. However, if approached in a businesslike manner, your friends can become wonderful sources of business. These new agents also tell me that their former business acquaintances have been great sources of business—because their former business associates look at them as competent business people, trusting the skills developed in former careers to carry over to real estate sales.

Do not think that you can simply mail out an announcement that you have just entered real estate—and expect your friends or business acquaintances to call you. You must develop a system and dialogue to call these people and ask for leads. Assisting you as you develop these systems and dialogues is a part of the service your mentor or manager can provide to you.

A caveat about "built-in" contacts: Even though it can be easier to get started in an area where you have social and business contacts, it is more important to *go out and make sales calls*. I found this to be true time after time, as I watched (and assisted) people in building their careers. Mark had grown up in the community where he wanted to sell real estate. In the banking business for 15 years, he developed many business contacts. Still, when he went into real estate, he sat around and complained that people he knew kept doing business with other real estate salespeople. I offered to help Mark make contacts with his sphere of influence—all those social and business people he knew. But, Mark refused to make a list of these people. After listening to Mark complain for several weeks, I helped Mark make a career change. In contrast, Tim moved into an area where he had no contacts. He went right out and made hundreds of sales calls. Within one month, he had sold two houses! Now, in his first six months in the business, he has completed 12 transactions!

Location   About where you live: As a manager, I watched agents attempt to start real estate careers in areas far removed from where they lived, which proved difficult for them. By the time they commuted a half-hour to their real estate office, it was too far out of the area they were familiar with. So, if you plan to start your real estate career in a market area outside where you live, plan to move into that area.

Property Type   What type and price range of properties do you want to specialize in? Do you want to help first-time buyers? Do you relate to move-up or transferred buyers? What kind of properties do these people buy? Do you own a condominium and want to specialize in them? After deciding what type of buyers and properties you prefer, drive through the areas where these properties are located. Look at the "For Sale" signs in the area. Which companies specialize in the type of property you want to list and sell?

Why Not Specialize in Expensive Properties?   New agents sometimes tell me that they only want to list and sell very expensive properties. They're thinking "prestige" and "lots of commission dollars." But, as I look at the price range of properties that consistently sell, I find that it is generally the low to mid-price range of any market area. The higher the price range, the longer the market time.

There is lots of competition for the expensive-property market from experienced, successful agents who have worked their way into that market over a period of years, starting when their customers and clients were buying starter homes. As you will find out, listing agents marketing prestige homes must spend thousands of dollars of their own money to promote these properties. But, on average, less than one-quarter of the listings in an area's top price range sell in half a year.

Most important, new agents need to make lots of people happy their first year in the business in order to create powerful referral and return businesses. Although one $8,000 commission looks great, one or two happy customers per year does not help you build a dynamic referral business.

Choosing An Area New to You　If you are new to town, drive around the various areas. Note the kind of homes in each area. Ask yourself, "Would my natural social circle live in these types of homes? Would I feel comfortable listing and selling this type of property?" New agents worry too much about not having social contacts if they are new to the area. Remember, "it's not who we know; it's who we contact consistently" that builds our business. Starting out in real estate and new to Seattle, I knew two people (not counting the grocery clerk and the dry cleaners). My boss told me to go out and talk to people. Taking orders well, I did just that. Within a week, I sold a home. Others in my office sold only one home a year! As I became an experienced agent, I realized that these "once a year" salespeople were really "secret agents." They knew lots of people, but just refused to talk to them about their real estate needs.

Other Sources of Information　For more information concerning particular companies and offices, look in the local phone book to contact the local multiple listing service and the local Association of REALTORS®. The multiple listing service can give you the number of offices in the company, the location of the offices, and the number of agents in a particular office. The Association of REALTORS® can give you additional information about offices in the area. They will probably refer you to active local NAR members, so you can talk with them about their companies and offices.

After choosing five or six offices, query people inside and outside the business to get the kind of perspective many agents only get after they have affiliated, which is a little late.

Title Companies, Mortgage Companies, Banks, Builders Call several people who regularly do business with these five or six real estate companies for an inside view on how those companies treat their customers. Ask them about the level of professionalism, the company's strengths, specialties, weaknesses and challenges. Ask them for their recommendations and the reasons. Ask them to recommend particular managers or owners and the reasons. Remember to ask enough people so that you do not rely on one person's opinion.

Get Agents' Opinions On Saturday or Sunday, buy a local newspaper and circle some "open house" newspaper ads. These ads will have addresses, so you can drive to the open house in the area where you want to work. Visit with agents holding these houses open. Ask them how they like their offices, why they joined that particular office, the specialties of that office and about their manager. Note the level of professionalism that the agent demonstrates:

- Is the level of material available in the home graphically pleasing? Does it look professional?
- Is the property prepared properly for an open house? Is it clean, does it smell fresh and is it ready for company?
- Does the agent have the professional appearance and demeanor with which you would want to be associated?
- Observe the agent's sales skills. Where was the agent when you entered the home? How is the agent dealing with the potential prospects? This will show you a lot about the manager's selection and training of the agents in that office.

Ask Customers and Clients As you shop for groceries, take your dry-cleaning, and eat in restaurants in your desired market area, ask those you come in contact with about their experiences with the real estate companies on your list. Find out about their experiences with particular agents. Ask for customers' recommendations for offices and good agents.

Study Companies' Advertising   Real estate companies advertise in several media (newspapers, television, radio, etc.) for two reasons: to advertise their products (their listed properties) and to communicate their image. Watch and listen to all the types of media coverage each company uses.

Gather all the paper advertising and mailings of each company. Put it on your table and look at it. Ask yourself, "From what I see, does this company know who it is? Does it project a consistent image? Do its signs, television and radio ads, mailers and other promotional pieces speak with one voice? What impression do they want me to have about them through this advertising?"

Match Your Desired Business to the Advertised Market Areas
Study the general price range and type of properties advertised. Will your area of specialty be supported with these advertising efforts? If you intend to list properties in one price range, and the company advertising features a completely different price range, your efforts will not be supported by the company.

Evaluate the Companies You Prefer

Now, put all your impressions of the company together—its agents, the perceptions of its customers, its product and image advertising, its perceived persona. How do they add up? Can you see yourself in this company? Figure 7.1 is a checklist to help narrow the choices in your preliminary search for the right office to the three to five companies you will want to contact for an interview.

Figure 7.1   Checklist Starting Your Real Estate Search

Affiliations
- ☐ None
- ☐ Regional
- ☐ National
- ☐ Other networks

Evaluation: _____

_____

Specialties
- ☐ Products
- ☐ Services
- ☐ Markets serviced

Evaluation: _____

_____

Company image
- ☐ Newspaper advertising
- ☐ Signs
- ☐ Radio, television
- ☐ Office
- ☐ Other

Evaluation: _____

_____

Agents
- ☐ Professional demeanor
- ☐ Sales skills

Evaluate: How your background, style, people you know fit the profile of this company: _____

_____

Other affiliated businesses
- ☐ Title companies
- ☐ Escrow companies
- ☐ Mortgage companies
- ☐ Attorneys
- ☐ Banks
- ☐ Builders
- ☐ Customers/clients

Evaluation: _____

_____

Summary

This chapter presents lots of tips on how to begin your search for the right real estate office for you. Important ideas are:

- In the nineties, new variations on the theme of affiliation will make it more challenging for agents to pick the right company and office for them.
- The company affiliations are important but less important than the suitability of particular office and manager.
- Gathering information from many sources within and outside of the business makes choosing the right office much easier.
- Taking time to match a company's image with your own professional image ensures that you will get the right advantages as you start your career.

8 What To Expect in the Interview

"Choose your company carefully. Moving from one company to another is costly to your business both in cost of your personal marketing materials and your image of stability. Factors to consider are the company's reputation in the community, presence in the market (market share), values that agree with your own and an office with an atmosphere where you feel you will easily fit in."

—Connie Walsh, five-year agent, former chef (once worked with Julia Child)

In This Chapter . . . .

- How to arrange for an interview
- How to prepare for the interview
- Your goals for the interview
- What your interviewer is looking for
- How to interview the interviewer
- Getting the rest of the story

. . . .

You are getting closer to the reality of real estate sales. Your next step will be to interview for a sales position. Throughout this book, I have told you that real estate sales practice is widely varied—from city to city, street to street—and from agent to agent. You will see this in the interview process. Some managers will ask you to take part in two-to-four-part interviews. Some will attempt to hire you after a five-minute chat! This chapter gives you norms and tips on how you can manage the interview process to get all the information you need to make a good decision.

Time Frame for Interviewing

The complete interview process can take from one day to several weeks. Figure 8.1 shows you the flow and time frame for a typical interview process. Most managers do not interview until the interviewee is scheduled for his license exam or has passed the exam. You should start interviewing seriously about three weeks before you take your exam. Why? You will want time to schedule:

Figure 8.1   The Interview Process

---

1. Make appointment for the first interview.
    *   Take your resume
    *   Prepare questions to ask
    *   Bring a notebook to record answers
    *   Manager may ask you to complete an application.

2. First interview, approximately one hour
    *   Manager asks questions to qualify you.
    *   Agent gathers information, asks questions.
    *   Manager makes appointment for second interview (if mutually agreeable).

OUR RECOMMENDATION: Request a second interview. Don't let yourself be hired at the first interview.

3. After the first interview
    *   Evaluate manager's interview process, organizational skills, materials used.
    *   If manager thinks you aren't a match in the office, manager won't set a second interview.

4. Second interview, approximately one hour
    *   Interviewer/manager exchange questions/information.
    *   Manager asks for affiliation, or
    *   Manager asks for more information (visit your home, meet spouse, or further interview).

5. Decision

- Initial appointments with the three to five offices you have chosen
- Second appointments with those offices
- Fact-gathering about those offices

As you choose a particular office, follow the process suggested here. Too often, an interviewee gets excited about what he hears in an interview and is flattered at being offered a position quickly. Hearing a great sales job, the interviewee quickly joins an office before gathering enough information to make the best choice, and later finds out that he or she didn't get the whole story. Next to your decision to make real estate your career, choosing your office and manager is the most important decision you will make. It can determine the success of your career.

Arrange for the Interview

Call the managers of the offices in which you are interested. Ask for an appointment. During the scheduling of that appointment, find out the time frame for that appointment, so you can plan your schedule. As a manager, I usually schedule an initial 45-minute interview. Ask the manager if you should send any materials prior to the interview and which materials, if any, you should bring to the interview. Some managers like to have a resume sent or an application completed and in the manager's hands prior to the first interview.

Why Written Information? As a manager, I want to find out three things:

1. Does the interviewee have writing skills?
2. Will the interviewee take orders by filling out the forms?
3. What information on the application needs to be expanded in that interview?

I can do a much better interview when I review the information on an application, find the areas of concern and perceive the strengths of the interviewee. This information helps to zero in on important areas of discussion, saving time for the interviewee and me.

Figure 8.2 shows you the information in a typical real estate application.

Figure 8.2 In a Real Estate Application

Personal information, such as:
- Name
- Address
- Phone

Real estate experience, such as:
- Licensing in another state
- Sales activity

General information, such as:
- Why real estate as a career
- Earnings expectations
- Why affiliate with this company

Work history, such as:
- Employer name, address
- Job description
- Income, reason for leaving

Education history, such as:
- School, years
- College, years
- Course of study

Personal references:
- Name, address
- Relationship, profession

Phone Screening Questions In order to save time and prescreen applicants, many managers ask preliminary questions over the phone. Some common ones are: "Do you intend to work in real estate as your main source of income? Have you already passed your license exam?" Compare these initial processes among the offices you choose.

If you have interviewed for a position in a different field or have been an interviewer, compare the professionalism of the process in these real estate offices with the processes previously experienced. The real estate manager with the best initial system will most likely carry that philosophy through other management practices. A well-thought-out screening system indicates care in picking agents to work with. Such a manager will spend more time with each person hired, to assure each new agent of getting a great start toward a dynamic career. One of the best and most successful owners I know has a four-part screening process. If you pass all of those criteria, you know you have been picked to be a part of a very special, successful group of people. Predictably, that manager has a top-producing office with little turn-over.

After the Call Send a note to thank the manager for his or her time, and say you're looking forward to the interview. Some weeks, I have five to seven interviews. The person who writes a note is always more impressive, and I assume that the interviewee will follow up on clients and customers just as attentively as with me.

Prepare for the Interview

First, your clothes. As you interview other agents in visits to their open houses, note how they are dressed. Do they look as though they are ready and qualified to help customers and clients spend hundreds of thousands of dollars? Or, do they look as though real estate is something they fit in between recreational pursuits? Even if you find that the real estate salespeople in your area and/or your desired office dress casually, you should dress for your interview in a conservative, businesslike manner. That means, for men, a conservative shirt, jacket and tie (unless you are in a very casual market area, and no one, including the owner of the company, ever wears ties and jackets). For women, a conservative suit or skirt and jacket. No very short skirts, no flashy jewelry, no heavy make-up, eye-catching hose or evening shoes. Bring a reasonable-size purse and/or briefcase.

Conservative—Why? Because potential customers and clients judge you in the first few seconds they see you. They ask themselves whether they believe you are the type of person to whom they can entrust their money. As you interview, pretend the manager is your customer, which is true because you are selling *yourself*. Be sure you are well groomed, with carefully washed, combed and cut hair, trimmed nails, and polished shoes and briefcase or purse. One of the biggest concerns managers grapple with is, "How can I tactfully teach my agents to dress more appropriately for the office?" The best way to solve that sensitive problem is to hire agents who already understand the importance of conservative, appropriate business dress. The truth of the matter is, the more the manager perceives you as a problem, the less he or she will want to hire you. Remove all barriers to getting hired!

Your Car Be sure your car is clean—outside and inside. Observant managers find out what car you drive, or will drive in real estate, and its condition. I'll never forget the day I got into an agent's car to inspect a property. I had not seen her car before (not smart). That car looked like a little garbage dump—and it was old garbage. It struck me like a bolt of lightning that that car absolutely represented our company image to the buyer who got into it (and probably got into it only once).

What to Take to the Interview Bring along your resume or application, even if you sent them prior to the interview. Managers are human. They have been known to lose resumes. If you bring a resume, be sure your resume addresses real estate sales specifically. When I read resumes that are general, I think that the interviewee is shopping for an occupation. Your resume should be short, concise and easy to read. If you are unsure about how to write your resume, check out one of the many excellent books available on how to create an effective resume. Be aware: Managers are looking for the traits they think are important—not for a list of credentials. This chapter will show you the qualities and the behaviors managers value.

Complete Assignments—Shows Positive Sales Traits Be sure to complete any assignments the manager has given you, such as completing the application. I want that application and questionnaire at least one hour prior to my interview, so I can prepare my interview. When the interviewee shows up with application in hand—or an incomplete application—I conclude that the interviewee is not much interested in becoming affiliated with us. From my tone, you can probably guess that one of the qualities I want to see demonstrated by the applicant's behavior is *accountability*. I use that application process to see whether the interviewee comes through on his promise to complete and send the paperwork prior to the interview. If not, will he or she carry through on promises to a customer or client?

Your Goal for the Interview You have two objectives:

1. Gather information.
2. Sell yourself.

The Manager's Goal for the Interview The manager also has two objectives:

1. Gather information.
2. Sell the company, office and himself

Who Asks Questions First? Both you and the manager have the same objectives. Who gets to ask questions first? Good managers take control of the interview process by asking questions to *qualify the interviewee first*. Then, after finding out whether that agent is qualified to join their office, they answer questions and sell the interviewee on the benefits of joining the office. That is just good sales technique. Would you put a customer in your car before you found out that they could buy—and that they were the kind of person you wanted to work with? Qualifying to buy always precedes selling. If the process is reversed, the salesperson can end up selling something to someone who may not want to buy it—or may not be qualified to buy it. Let the manager take the lead. You will get indicators of his or her sales skill, and you can establish rapport through a cooperative attitude.

Figure 8.3 shows that the agent's process in qualifying, showing and closing customers is exactly the same process managers use in qualifying agents.

Figure 8.3 The Sales Process

Agent Customer Sales Process		Manager Interview Process
	QUALIFY	
1. Agent qualifies customer.		Manager qualifies agent.
	SELL BENEFITS	
2. Agent shows homes.		Manager shows benefits (to customer agent) of joining office.
	CLOSE	
3. Agent closes customer.		Manager closes agent.

What the Manager Looks for Good interviewers ask you lots of questions to discover:

- Your motivation to succeed (must match the office expectations)
- The traits and characteristics you bring to real estate that match the office profile

Figure 8.4 shows you the qualities that I value when I hire associates.

Questions to Expect Early in the Interview Figure 8.5 lists questions with the traits and qualities that they indicate. These are the kinds of questions skilled interviewers ask. They are termed *behavioral-based questions* because they ask the interviewee to recall his past behavior. Because we know that people will behave in the future as they did in the past, behavioral-based questions give us the best indicators of a person's relative strengths of character and how they will apply these strengths in sales.

General Interviewing Tips If you feel that you need to brush up on your interviewing skills, consult one of the excellent sources available today:

Figure 8.4 Qualities of a Real Estate Office Associate

---

1. *High personal initiative:* Your success depends on your being able to create programs and implement them on your own with relatively little monitoring.

2. *Tenacity:* Only those who stick with it will win. Plan on dedicating one year to establishing your business.

3. *Mental toughness:* A positive mental attitude is essential. Others who give up easily will try to influence the tenacious, mentally tough individual to also give up. It takes courage to keep going in this long-term business.

4. *Belief in oneself:* We each have to know, inside ourselves, that we are capable, that we have the talent and tenacity to succeed, and can depend on ourselves.

5. *Willingness to take direction:* Real estate is a constantly changing field. Those who win and keep building a stronger business learn new skills and apply them consistently.

6. *Enthusiasm:* A joy in doing and a desire to accomplish show up in an enthusiastic attitude.

7. *Creativity:* In today's market-oriented world, an agent must be truly creative to design programs where he or she stands out as valuable and different.

8. *Educated and communicative:* Writing skills are a necessity today. Our sophisticated target markets are well educated. Effective verbal communication is also paramount to success.

- Go to the library to get a book on interviewing.
- Take a course at a community college in job hunting, resume writing and/or interviewing skills.
- Hire a career counselor.

The Day of the Interview

Arrive ten minutes early. Before you go into the manager's office, note:

- Exterior of office—maintenance: What does that say about the image of the office/company?

Figure 8.5 Behavioral-Based Questions

---

1. Describe a situation in your life where you failed miserably. Everyone told you that you should never attempt that again. How did you handle that failure—and what did you do next?
   Answer indicates relative tenacity and mental toughness, belief in oneself.

2. Describe a time in your life when you took a personal risk. What happened?
   Answer indicates amount of personal initiative.

3. Describe a time in your life when you went out to get a job. How did you go about it?
   Answer indicates ability to make sales calls, sell yourself.

- Demeanor of the receptionist and other support staff: Are they friendly, attentive, courteous?
- Interior of office: Is it clean and neat? Pretend you are a potential customer. Are you made comfortable? Would you be proud to have your customers come in?
- Atmosphere of office: Are agents relaxing (not very professional) in the reception area? Is the office humming with activity?
- Are you given information about the office and the company prior to going into the interview, so you feel more comfortable with the process?

Some managers prepare a company/office portfolio showing the features, benefits and services that they provide. This portfolio may be given to the prospective agent prior to the interview or used in the interview. As a manager, I find that interviewees who read our portfolio are impressed with all the services we offer. It speaks for us, raises our credibility and gives the interviewee a much better sense of our essence. This is the sales strategy that successful agents are using around the nation to introduce and promote themselves to potential customers and clients.

Your Turn: Get Information

After the initial questioning period, led by the manager, you are ready to ask questions. Figure 8.6 lists categories and specific questions in those categories. *Be sure to get a written description of the programs and statistics provided in the interview.* Otherwise, hearing the manager's sales pitch, you may conclude that the programs described in your interview are different or more developed than they, in fact, really are.

This happened to Anne, a prospective agent whom I interviewed. She told me that all the companies she interviewed with so far had told her that they had training programs. She also felt flattered that all of them asked her to join them after talking with her only a few minutes. Because I did not immediately hire her, Anne decided to join one of those other offices, where she had already been "sold and hired." This was the conversation she overheard on her first day at the office: Manager to assistant manager: "Hey, George. We've got a new agent. Are we going to do a training program?" George: "Nah. We don't have enough people to pay that guy from the island to come over." Disillusioned, Anne came back to our office, got our training program in writing, got the training program schedule and affiliated with us.

Because you will interview at more than one office, be sure to write down your answers. Use one checklist (Figure 8.6) for each office.

What's in it for Me? Find out the "what," the "how," and the "why it will benefit you" of every program mentioned by the manager. Do not be afraid to ask probing questions about a program you don't understand. In fact, the biggest mistake interviewees make is in not asking for a clarification and visual of a particular program. Remember, managers are salespeople. You will need to remain focused on your questions to avoid being swept up in the emotion of the moment. You have answered all the manager's questions. Now, it's your turn. Take your time!

How to End the Initial Interview Some managers attempt to "close" the interviewee at the end of the first interview. Unless you are very comfortable with the manager and the office, express your interest and ask to get back together with the manager within the next few

Figure 8.6 Interview Topics and Questions

GETTING ME STARTED IN THE OFFICE

- Manager's program
- Orientation packet/checklists
- Checklist for operations
- Business plan
- Mentors
- Schedule for me

- What systems do you have to get agents started fast?
- How do you work with me to ensure my success?
- What are your success statistics? How will you acclimate me to the office and to the business of real estate?

EDUCATION/TRAINING

- Philosophy about
- Initial postlicense courses
- Advanced courses
- Clock hours
- Course schedule
- Course descriptions
- Who trains/qualifications

- Please explain how your education or training program helps me get started fast. Provide me statistics of new people and when they made their first sale.
- How is your program different from others?

THE OFFICE

- Office profile
- Statement of purpose
- Specializations
- Target markets
- Agent turnover—why?
- Desks/office space
- Customer/client profile
- Operations book
- Teams/task forces
- Earning potential
- Part-timers?

How many transactions, on average, do new agents complete here in their first year? What are your minimum production standards for a new agent for his first year? For all agents? Are there agents here who aren't reaching minimum requirements? How many? What does the average productivity of each agent mean to me?

Figure 8.6   Interview Questions (Continued)

IN-OFFICE HELP

- Manager availability
- Assistant manager
- Secretarial help
- Library

- Advisors
- Office portfolio
- Office training
- Resources
- Machinery

> How do managers, assistant managers and/or advisers support me? Please give me a tour of your office and point out the resources you have.

SUPPORT FOR PRODUCTIVITY

- Personal promotion materials— strategy
- Scheduling: floor time/open house
- Best sources of business

- Referrals—how handed out?
- Advertising policies
- Paper supplies

> How will you help me promote myself? Get a list of all the materials and services provided by the company. Get a list of the materials and services provided by the agent. Get costs involved.

MANAGEMENT

- Background
- Education/training
- Strengths
- Communication between agents/manager

- Advanced designations
- Do you sell?
- Philosophy on hiring

> Describe your management style. What's important to you? Where do you see real estate in three years? Ten years? How do you get new information? How do you communicate it? What are you doing differently this year? Why?

Figure 8.6   Interview Questions (Continued)

COMPANY PROFILE

- Philosophy
- Programs
- Challenges
- Company report
- Stance on agency

- Mission statement
- Print materials
- Future
- Affiliations
- REALTOR® company?

> What is the company known for? What is it really good at? Why should I join you?

MARKETING STRATEGIES

- Institutional (image-making)
- Community service strategies

- Media used and why
- Public relations

> Explain your marketing strategies as a company, and the philosophy behind them. Explain ad policies. Who pays for the ads?

SERVICES PROVIDED

- Errors and omissions insurance
- Attorney services
- Answering service
- Group rates on services

- Health, dental plans
- Retirement plans
- Relocation

> Why are these important? How are they different from other companies?

GROWING MY CAREER

- Programs
- Business planning—how?

- Management help for growth opportunities

> What opportunities are there in your firm for my long-term career growth? Related career opportunities (teaching, mentoring, managing, etc.)?

Figure 8.6 Interview Questions (Continued)

COMMISSION SCHEDULES

- Description
- Philosophy behind
- Operation of
- Exceptions to

Do you make some exceptions to your commission schedule—and, if so, why?

days. Why? Because you want to get enough information to *be sure of your decision*. At the end of this interview, it is appropriate to ask to see the office. Note the work spaces, support services and mechanical support, such as computers. Look at the layout of the office. Where would your desk be? Is it a "bull pen" configuration? Are desks shared? How are desk assignments determined? You can find out a lot about management philosophy by analyzing the answers to these questions. Meet some of the agents, if possible. What is their attitude about another new person? Are they cordial?

Other Ways To Gather Information

- Ask to attend an office meeting. That can really be revealing and is essential, I think.
- Ask to go on an office tour of new listings. Ride with some experienced agents, and ask them questions about the office, company and manager. You may get a grumbler or two, but every office has a few.
- Ask the manager for the names of two or three agents who have been with the office less than six months. Call them and ask, "How did you get started? What were the biggest challenges you faced? How did the manager help you? If you could do something differently, what would it be?"
- Go out and inspect the office inventory with the manager. Be sure to ask, "How did that agent get that listing?"
- Request a list of agents in that office and ask which ones you should talk to. Talk to those people, but also talk to others on the list—the more, the better. Ask the experienced agents about the office organization, hiring philosophy and their feelings about the office. Is there challenge and encouragement for professional growth?
- Interview with the owner of the company, if possible (if he or she is not also the manager). As the leader, that person sets the tone for the entire company. You need to feel that his or her vision is closely related to your career goals.

What To Expect in the Second Interview

Generally, the second interview is much less formal, with both parties asking questions and exchanging information. I love second interviews, because that is when I really get to know the interviewee—and I think the interviewee really gets comfortable with the office and me. Then, the agent is less apt to have *buyer's remorse*—the free-floating anxiety that you feel when you fear having made a bad decision.

In real estate sales, agents have to deal frequently with customers and clients who suffer buyer's remorse. Good agents help buyers avoid buyer's remorse by providing adequate information, counseling and support during the buying process. Then, when buyers are ready to make a buying decision, they feel competent, confident and excited about going ahead to sign on the dotted line. Good managers are as sensitive to interviewees as good agents are to their customers and clients. We managers want to be sure the interviewee is as sold on us as we are on them. That avoids buyer's remorse.

What if the Manager Doesn't Want To Interview You Again?

If the manager does not feel that you match the profile of the agents of the office, the manager will decline to interview you again. He or she may send you a letter after the first or second interview, thanking you for the opportunity to interview and telling you that he feels you would match the profile of another office better than his.

This determination is in your best interests. It would be a disservice to you to go to an office that is not the best for you. The manager who cares about the tone of his office—and about the interviewee—has the foresight to make those tough choices.

What if You Are Asked To Join the Office?

At any time during the first or second interview, you may be asked to join the office. If you are not sure about the office, simply tell the manager that you are not ready to make a decision. If you know, at that time, that you do not want to join that office, tell the manager that you do not think this office and you are a career match. The manager will appreciate your candor. No manager wants to hire someone who is not sold on the office and the manager.

Match Production Goals

Some interviewees think that, even though they are not committed to real estate as careerists, they should find the most productive company and office with which to affiliate. They assume that the tone and productivity of the office will given them some easy money. Unfortunately, that thinking leads to a mismatch in goals and expectations. Managers who hire careerists have high standards for productivity. They have highly refined systems to help agents get started fast in their careers. And, these managers are not prepared to manage the less committed agent. This mismatch will lead to frustration for both parties. It is very important to be honest and clear about your career goals and to affiliate with an office and manager who reflect similar goals. That ensures a great start for both agent and manager.

You're Hired!

At the end of the second interview, the manager looks at you and says, "Jody, we'd really like to have you join our office. You'd be a wonderful addition to our team." You graciously accept the offer. Now, what happens? The manager will explain the steps that you'll take together to:

1. activate your real estate license,
2. orient you to the office and
3. register you in training school.

Then, the manager will explain the start-up program for you for your first week in the business. Generally, you will be doing these activities:

- Generating leads to develop your business (prospecting activities)
- Organizing your real estate materials
- Previewing property
- Sending out new agent announcements
- Learning the computer and other mechanical equipment in the office

- Acclimating yourself to all resource information, files and forms in the office

This is where those orientation checklists mentioned in your interview questions come in really handy. Do not expect your manager to work closely with you these first few days. You will probably be given a simple list of things to accomplish, and you will be expected to complete the assignments alone. Charlie Deardorff, a very successful agent now in his third year, found that first week in business one of the most baffling times in his life. With literally no guidance, he found himself muttering, "Now I'm licensed. Now what do I do?" Charlie's advice to new agents is to choose an office that provides a specific, well-defined orientation checklist and a list of tasks to be accomplished that first week. Without that guidance, Charlie says, it is very easy to sit around the office watching agents get phone calls—and wonder how to get one. (One agent even had his spouse call him at the office—so he could feel he had gotten a call.)

Summary

This chapter takes you through the interview process. Important points are:

- Prepare yourself for the interview to make a favorable first impression—the key to being chosen by a discriminating office.
- Realize that some managers don't qualify prospects. They *sell* prospects. Do not be flattered at a quick offer of a job. Instead, take your time.
- Take advantage of all the ways you have to get information. And, get visual proof of the claims you hear from your interviewer.

9 Off to a Fast Start—And Beyond

"I had been in real estate about four months, and was trying to continue my contracting business while I sold real estate. Another agent in the office told me that I needed to drop my pursuit of other work and get focused. I listened to him, and from that day forward my business took off."

—Lisa Mundahl, first-year top-producing agent, former building contractor

In This Chapter . . . .

- Setting your posture for success
- Crafting a productive career
- Career horizons
- Space-age trends

. . . .

It is difficult to write about real estate as a career without actually giving directions on how to do the job every day. But, that's a "how to create a successful career—your first year" book. Limiting this book to answering the questions you have as a prospective agent means my "successful career" book will have to be a sequel to this one. For now, an excellent book on selling real estate that contains lots of information you will need as you start your career, is *Your Successful Real Estate Career*, by Kenneth W. Edwards, updated in its 1993 edition. One of the most helpful parts of the book for new agents is its section on recordkeeping and tax preparation.

Your Posture for Success

As you were growing up, did your mother correct your posture? "Stand up straight. You're slumping." Mine did, too. I guess all mothers go to the "mother's training school," where they learn those directives that we all get as we grow up—and that we pass on dutifully to our off-spring. And, all of us, as caring parents, remind our children about their posture because we care about them. We don't want them to grow up stooped and unable to make the most of their lives. That reminder about posture, and the thought behind it, is really apt for beginning your real estate sales career. Too many agents go into the field not really "standing up straight." They have other jobs, too many obligations and not enough commitment to succeeding in their real estate career. They're really not "standing up straight," facing the job as a real career change. Rather, they look at real estate sales as a diversion or avocation. And, they are finding out, like Lisa, that making a successful career of real estate sales requires full commitment.

Brokers Can Help Change Posture

Just as mothers set the standards for physical posture (for our own good), brokers can set the standards for their agents' "financial posture" (for the agents' benefit). Brokers have a responsibility to disclose in the interview the truths of the business to prospective agents, so agents will be able to plan financially for their business. Also, prospective agents need understanding and guidance at the outset to help them avoid wasting their savings, by helping them create very successful careers. But, let's look at the financial picture, not only from the agents' perspective, but from the broker's. In the past, real estate brokers could make a profit by affiliating with agents who regarded real estate as an avocation. But, with the generous commission splits and the higher brokerage costs of the past few years, brokers can no longer afford to hire "avocationers" and keep nonproductive people. In fact, the National Association of REALTORS® 1991 survey of real estate brokerage firms showed that profits of real estate companies were steadily declining. From an analysis of these firms, NAR stated that increasing each agents productivity was the key to profitability in the nineties. So, the nineties is the era when change will occur—because, to be profitable, real estate brokerage firms must change in order to stay in business. As we all know, change is hard. Looking at their bottom lines, real estate brokers realize that, to make a profit, they must hire and work only with committed, productive agents. But, "realizing" and "doing" are two different things. Old habits die hard. We are in a transition period. Here are some of the ways brokers can help to change the posture of the industry—for your benefit:

Enhance the Interviewing and Screening Process Chatting with hundreds of brokers across the nation, I have found that few managers use any written screening devices (applications, aptitude profiles, etc.). They seem to do more selling than questioning. New agents characterize their interviews as sales jobs. These practices lead to turnover in the industry. Yet, necessity is the mother of invention. Brokers are realizing that productive agents create a profitable office. So, as brokers realize what a nonproductive agent costs them, they will adopt much better screening devices in the rest of this decade. (As I teach across the nation, I ask brokers what a nonproductive agent costs them. Most don't know, so I have developed a questionnaire to help them figure this out. From their estimates, the range of costs for hiring an agent who does not get productive within six months is $15,000 to $40,000!)

Set Production Standards for New and Experienced Agents Some brokers still allow agents to have "bad posture"— to come into their offices with low commitment and stay there even when the agents have not been productive enough to pay the costs the broker has incurred to have that agent there. Why does the broker keep the person? Because, in the past, other agents in the office, through their productivity, could "subsidize" the cost of the incompetent agent. Now, brokers are just realizing that this subsidy arithmetic does not compute in today's climate. Now, each agent must "pay his own freight." Think of it this way: As you affiliate with your office, you immediately become, to your broker, a one-person potential profit center. This is the way your broker must look at you to keep the office doors open (make a profit) in the nineties. When brokers divide their total monthly expenses by the number of desks available in their offices, they find it costs from $800 to $1,500 per month for each desk in an office. In most offices, the agent does not pay this fee per month by giving his broker a check, as is the case in "desk fee" offices. Instead, agents "pay" the broker by selling enough property to return expenses and profit to ownership—each month. Could some great, experienced agent subsidize your start in your career by earning more dollars to pay to the broker for your desk while you learn the business? Not in the nineties. Because of the nature of commission agreements between agents and ownership, the broker does not capture enough commission dollars from productive agents to subsidize a nonproductive agent. That is why brokers today want to help agents get a fast start. It is beneficial to both the agent and the broker.

Set Expectations for New Agents for Business-Producing Activities, Time Frames and Income   Joan, a manager of a 20-person office, was disappointed with Mark, an agent in her office, because he had made no sales in the year he had been there. Why had she not terminated Mark's contract, to help him go on to another career where he could be more successful? Joan told me that, she thought, given enough time, that Mark would sell something. Many brokers started in real estate in a different era, when expenses of both the agent and the broker were low. So, agents and broker could afford to take the attitude that, in time, an agent can catch on. However, my survey with new agents revealed that the largest group of new agents expected to make a sale their first month in the business. About half of the respondents could go less than six months without a check before leaving the business. What's going on? Managers are managing new agents the way the manager was managed as an agent. But, it is a different era now. Agents coming into the business have different expectations. Smart managers are matching expectations in the interview, showing agents how certain business plans ensure that the agent reaches his expectation, and getting the agent's commitment to work the plan. Managers also must share their income expectations of that new agent for his first year. My survey showed that the largest group of new agents expected to make $31,000 to $75,000 their first year in real estate. (Remember the median income for a REALTOR®? $22,500.) However, only 1 in 16 (71 percent of the agents surveyed had no idea of how many transactions they needed to complete to stay affiliated with their office) know what their manager's expectations of them were!

A trend of the nineties: Managers will share income expectations with new agents in the interview, so that the new agent can compare his or her expectations to the manager's minimum expectations of the agent. Managers will become much more numbers-oriented, so that the new agent has a clear picture of what is expected of him or her. In the nineties, savvy agents will not feel comfortable investing "themselves" in a real estate office without those measurable projections, either.

How To Craft a Productive Career

Back to your posture, then. How can you, with your determination for career success, assure that you are getting, and staying, on the right track? I asked some very successful agents—those who created strong careers in their first year—to give you some advice. Their comments stressed certain areas; they are grouped accordingly.

1. Get a good business-developing plan and work it consistently.

    From Brian Orvis: "If you don't prospect, the potential for failing in this business greatly increases. I wish I knew how to tell other agents, in a nice way, to get the hell out of my way when they try to discourage me from proactive prospecting (cold calls/phones, expired listings, for-sale-by-owners)."

    From Renee Menti: "Put yourself in front of buyers and sellers every day in some way."

    From Connie Walsh: "Write a business plan every year, allow for flexibility and live by it."

    And, from a survey of 50 very successful first-year agents, when I asked them what they wished they had had more of, they said "business planning." With a better plan for finding buyers and sellers, they thought they could have done better faster.

2. Devote enough time and energy to the business from day one to create the financial rewards you need to do this job.

   From Liz Talley: "Thank goodness that I love what I do because I do it about 12 hours a day. The lunches, dinners, shopping have gone. This job can be really, really busy. To me, making substantial money is tied directly to enjoying this job. Without the financial rewards, I know that my enthusiasm would drift."

3. Keeping the customers' best interests in mind pays dividends.

   From Lisa Mundahl: "Real estate sales carries a weight of responsibility similar to practicing law. Selling a person's home is an intimate affair. As salespeople we must recognize and respect the ego that is expressed in one's home. Be honest, be interested and be sincere."

   From Brian Orvis: "Never look at the end result (commission) before going into a listing presentation and expect to get the listing. People are more respectful of you when you are brutally honest about everything. In other words, don't give them the bunch of crap that flaky agents would use."

4. Keeping a positive attitude is up to you.

   From Charlie Deardorff: "Do not get caught up in what other agents in your office are doing. There is enough real estate business for everyone to make money."

   From Connie Walsh: "One of the realities of real estate is facing rejection. It is important to be a part of an office team that is positive."

   From Renee Menti: "I have some affirmations that I use daily to keep myself 'up.' One of them is, I have persistence, consistency, and a positive attitude."

You can do your own survey. As you start your career, find the most successful first-year agents in your company. Interview them to find out exactly what they did in their first few months in the business to assure fast, high results.

Secrets of Creating a Super-Career

Talk to Lots of People—Starting on Day One

Throughout this book, I have been telling you that going out and talking to hundreds of people to find qualified buyers and sellers—from your first day in the business—is critical to your career success. Am I coming across as a person who only cares about the money? Let's admit it. Making money in real estate is a most important measure of success and professionalism. Why? Because the reward for helping our customers and clients get what they want is that we get what we want—a commission check.

Get Recognition for Your Success—To Get More Success

When you get a sale quickly, you get noticed by management. Other people talk about you and compliment you on your success. All this attention and accomplishment make you feel good. When you feel good about yourself, you go out and do more of those things that cause you to feel good. Feeling good about ourselves, we can withstand the disappointments and rejections that occur in great numbers to all real estate agents—but especially to new agents.

Remember what Connie said about rejection? You're going to get lots of it in real estate. I know that. I was a college music teacher. When I went to a party, people asked me what I did for a living. I told them I taught piano and flute performance at the college level. Boy, were they respectful of me! My self-esteem soared. Then, I went into real estate sales. Same kind of people. Same type of party. Same question. Different answer: "I sell real estate." And a different reaction! People treated me less warmly. They were wary, less friendly, less respectful. For one of the few times in my life, I questioned my self-worth. I was still the same person I was when I taught music. I had not become unethical, hard-sell or untrustworthy. It took me a few months to figure out that, although the word salesperson has unsavory meaning to some people, it wasn't me. You will experience the same feelings. Every new salesperson does. However, as you progress in your career, and become known as a successful real estate salesperson, people will seek you out at parties—because they have learned through your actions, that you are an example of the best kind of salesperson—professional, caring and successful!

Recognize the Value of Self-Esteem to Your Success

Think about a time in your life when you were feeling great about yourself. You did something memorable, didn't you? Or, someone complimented you about something you did. Now translate that to real estate. What are the activities agents accomplish that are memorable? Selling homes, listing homes and selling those listings. Those are the results that are rewarded by companies through prizes, contests, trophies and acknowledgment in front of your peers. Those results take months to accomplish. Now, imagine that you have been at your office for almost one year and have sold only two homes. When you came into the business, you understood that you needed to find prospects to get results. But, after you made a few calls and experienced rejection, you felt bad, so you quit making those calls. You saw Josie sell a home that she had held open, so you figured that luck has a lot to do with real estate success. And, it is less frightening to sit at an open house and wait for a good buyer to come in—although, as you discovered after a few months, that only happens once or twice in a real estate salesperson's life. As is normal in a real estate office, you did the activities that you like to do each day, with no one monitoring your daily activities. After all, you are in business for yourself. After a few months of no results, your manager called you into his office and questioned you about your level of productivity. You explained that, you were very busy and that you thought you had some leads. The manager was glad to hear that you thought you were going to do better, and told you so. Unfortunately, as the months went by, those "leads" didn't pan out. As the year wore on, you got discouraged and looked down on yourself for lack of results. Experienced agents call this feeling of failure a slump. At the end of the year, you attend an honors meeting created by your company. Wolfgang, who started with you, is being honored as "Rookie of the Year" because he sold 15 homes. As Wolfgang goes up to the dais to accept his trophy to a standing ovation, how do you feel? It's the old self-esteem issue, right? Even though Wolfgang is your friend, and you are glad for him, you rationalize his greater success by speculating that he got leads from the manager, just lucked out in that open house and probably knows more people than you do. You would not want to think that Wolfgang's success resulted from doing the activities that you chose not to do.

Copy Success—If You Know What It Looks Like

Wolfgang's daily planner shows that he consistently talked to potential prospects every day. In fact, Wolfgang talked to hundreds of potential prospects each month. It is too late now to go back to that first year. You have spent thousands of dollars in savings and wasted a lot of time by starting your real estate career your way—the way that was easiest for you. Based on the measurements of success—sales results—you are a failure. Now, where is your self-esteem? That's right—in the dumper. I projected a year for you to help you get the feel of results-oriented rewards when you are not one of the people recognized.

Ensure That Your Enthusiasm Has Staying Power

It takes only three to four weeks without results (a sale or a listing) for a new agent to feel like a failure. My survey of new agents shows that a majority of agents expects to make a sale the first month in the business. That is why depression sets in so fast. What does that tell managers? That we had better help you new agents into a high-numbers, activity-based business-producing plan fast—or you will consider yourself a failure—fast. Also, you need lots of positive encouragement as you start your career. That encouragement, though, has a hollow ring to it unless it is based on what you did that day, that week, that month—to create business.

Give Yourself Enough Time To Succeed

The majority of new agents surveyed gave themselves less than six months to make it in the real estate business. They expect to create a dynamic, successful, high-income producing business right away —or they intend to get out. However, experienced agents tell us that it takes two to three years to really reap the rewards of their hard work. Why do those rewards come in years two and three? For one thing, the experienced agents have learned the best lessons of real estate through real life. They have become much better at providing customer satisfaction. They have honed their business skills and are more technically proficient. The prospects they met their first few months in the business have finally become serious buyers and sellers. By keeping in touch with these prospects, these agents have created a gold mine of prospects for future income. How many months or years have you given yourself to create a successful career? If you go out your first day in the business and start making sales calls, you can create a sale quickly. You will lay the groundwork for a great second year.

Be Uncomfortable—To Get Comfortable

No matter what agents did before entering real estate, most were comfortable and secure doing it. From the age of four, I tickled the ivories. When I started kindergarten, I accompanied my kindergarten class as they danced and sang. All through grade school, high school, college and graduate school I thought of myself, and others thought of me, as a musician. I was comfortable. Even if I did not know the answer to a musical question, I was secure saying, "I don't know." When I went into real estate, every third sentence I uttered seemed to be, "I don't know but I'll find out." I felt so inadequate. "Pianissimo and "fortissimo" just were not useful as real estate vocabulary. It took three years to get as comfortable in real estate sales as I had been as a musician. You, like me, will have to tolerate "not knowing."

The Silver Lining

Real estate is a performance art. Just like learning to drive a car, you are not as good at it the first time you do it as you are after experiencing life on the road. That first year in real estate is really life on the road. If you dive right in, as I suggest, not only will you make money fast, but you will learn the skill of real estate sales. You will become technically proficient (writing purchase and sale agreements, etc.), because you will immediately put the knowledge you learned in class to work. At the same time, you will experience great frustration, dejection and discouragement because of being new at selling real estate. Think of it this way: You might as well get this learning period over with fast. These lessons, learned now, are invaluable in creating a successful career.

Education Is Not the Only Determinant to Your Success

As a dutiful new agent, you will listen in class, do the exercises, memorize the terms, and think you are prepared to sell real estate. Then, real life on the road will show you how much you still have to learn. Most of that learning is in the people skills of real estate. How to meet people. How to get their names and an appointment. How to follow up to get an appointment to show them homes. How to get their loyalty. How to close them to sell them a home. How to deal with rejection, lack of respect and lack of loyalty unprecedented in your life (unless you were in commissioned sales). To even figure out what you need to learn, you must get right out into the action and fail a few times. Then, you will seek out the best way to find the answers to your people problems—a sales skills workshop—the kind of true training workshop I mentioned in an earlier chapter. Why? Because this is the only type of classroom environment that gets you close to real life. The frustrations agents experience can be dealt with best through their taking a great people-skill-enhancing workshop—with lots of role-play practice in class plus field work to further practice sales skills with real people. In the nineties, you will find much better sales skill training courses available to meet careerists' demands for the skills they need to create good careers.

How Your Manager Can Help

One of the most effective ways to get those people skills you need is to affiliate with a manager who is a trained trainer. That manager will most likely provide real skills training in the office. Shelly Nohre, a very successful manager and trainer in the Seattle area, provides weekly skill-building workshops for the agents in her office. Here is an example of her training workshops: Each agent who attends the workshop has prepared a specific presentation. This week, it is part of the listing presentation. One agent becomes the listing agent, while another agent acts as a seller. The listing agent actually gives this part of the listing presentation to the seller (another agent in the office). The seller (other agent) acts like a real seller during the time of the presentation. Afterward, the seller/agent gives constructive feedback to the listing agent, using a specific feedback format that Shelly devised. Then, the whole group discusses what they heard. They learn by coaching each other.

No wonder the agents in Shelly's office are good at listing properties and highly confident of their abilities. As a musician I know that "perfect practice makes perfect." I also know that I can't expect to give a good performance (a listing presentation in front of real sellers) without practicing my presentation several times, getting performance coaching from someone I trust. The best news is that I am much more confident of my ability to handle the sellers' concerns and objections because of my practice in dealing with them. Football teams do not play games without practice—and part of that practice is with simulated opponents. Real estate agents shouldn't perform real estate with real buyers and sellers until they practice with their manager or other competent coaches. Look for this to be a big trend of the nineties: skills training workshops provided by schools, companies and individual offices.

Patience Pays Off in Success

How many years will it be before I am as comfortable in my new life as I was in my old one? Successful, experienced agents tell me that it takes two to three years to build the career as envisioned—and to feel comfortable in that career. So, create a *three-year plan* for real estate success. When you begin your career with that commitment, you can reap the rewards that you work so hard to achieve. Many of the prospects you met in your first year will actually buy or sell with you in your second or third year if you keep in touch with them. According to customer surveys, it will take you six to eight contacts to form a rapport with a potential customer or client. That is why experienced agents find that years two and three are so financially and emotionally rewarding.

Become a Specialist

Successful agents have found the key to long-term success: Becoming a "specialist." Just as doctors invest in themselves to become specialists, agents today grow their careers dramatically by specializing. One agent who specializes in condominium projects calls himself the "condo king." All he does is list and sell condominium projects. So, if he finds a customer who wants to buy waterfront property, he refers him to a waterfront specialist. Agents are finding out that, to be memorable, you must be known for something. You cannot be known for everything. Consumers are learning to ask for a specialist. You can imagine that, if Mrs. Smith wants to sell her waterfront property, she does not want someone who sells homes mainly to first-time buyers or someone who dabbles in a little of everything. She wants a waterfront specialist. She will ask her friends to recommend someone. After hearing the same name a few times, she will call that agent. The consumer loves the specialist idea. As you refine your career, consider which specialty you want to be known for. It is the wave of the nineties.

Career Horizons

Becoming a good salesperson is the foundation for any specialty that you may decide to investigate as your sales career matures. Why? Because sales skill is the foundation for any successful specialty in the real estate field. New agents frequently told me, as a trainer for a very large real estate company, that they really didn't want to sell real estate. They really wanted to become a trainer, as I was. My advice to them was always the same: A sure way to become a good trainer is first to become a good real estate salesperson. That provides the experience and the credibility to become a specialist in other areas of real estate.

Managing an Assistant

Another trend of the nineties is successful, high-producing agents to hire an assistant. Hiring an assistant allows the agent more time to do the money-making activities. Many of these assistants have real estate licenses, so they can

- process listing and sales agreements,
- prepare and send out all personal marketing mailings,
- do prospecting calls and
- do all paperwork.

The Agent as Manager

High-producing agents today are learning to manage their activities so they can hire, train and work with an assistant. This means that the agent really has to be in business for himself or herself, skilled not only in self-management but in managing others. For many agents, this is a real challenge. Salespeople, generally, are not great organizers or planners. In the nineties, agents realize that, to reach higher production goals, they must be well organized and have a complete business plan (goals, strategies, tactics, time frames, work assignments and budget).Then, they can manage themselves and an assistant effectively. Working with assistants has enabled agents to create some dramatic income levels. A few agents today are grossing $500,000. However, their business expenses can range from one-third to one-half their gross amount.

Another job opportunity that some agents take is to become an assistant to a top agent. Assistants make from $12,000 to $40,000, depending on their experience and responsibilities. Generally, it is not strictly a salaried position, but salary plus bonuses based on the agent's income.

From Managing Yourself to Managing Many

As companies create more mega-offices, a new specialist emerges— the branch manager. This person is responsible for 40 to 100 salespeople in one office. He or she recruits, selects, trains and retains productive salespeople to make a profit in that office. In order to accomplish profitability, the branch manager must become a specialist in people management:

- Managing each person—helping each associate reach the monetary expectations shared by both the agent and the manager.
- Managing the group—creating a team of closely knit associates who agree on a mutually shared vision of their office.

One of the most challenging and exciting developments of the nineties is emergence of these branch manager specialists, for they are largely responsible for delivering a profit through the productivity of their people. New training programs especially designed for branch managers are now being introduced in the most creative companies to ensure that the services provided by the company are implemented for agents' benefits within the offices. To find experienced people managers, some companies are looking to other sales fields, where companies have long spent dollars and human resources to train their managers.

Want To Be An Entrepreneur?

For some agents and managers, the next logical step is into ownership. Today, because companies are offering franchise opportunities nationally, ownership of one or more offices can be an attractive opportunity. However, because profitability of real estate offices has been steadily declining, one must be an astute businessperson to deliver a profit for the office.

How About Becoming a Trainer?

As more and more companies affiliate with each other, and as offices grow larger, there will be a greater need for *training specialists*. According to the National Association of REALTORS® Horizon report of 1991, less than half of the companies surveyed say they have some kind of training programs. Only 11 percent of the firms have training for new sales associates. The need in the nineties is to raise each agent's productivity. The best way to do this is through training. So, much more attention will be paid to training—inside the office—and in the company—than ever before. And, agents will become more critical of their training programs. If they spend their time and money, they expect results. So, some of the loosely organized training sessions that sufficed in the past just won't pass muster anymore. Whether you become a trainer or not, you may consider sharing your expertise with new or experienced agents by becoming an instructor for your company's training program. Trainers always say, "We learn more teaching than the students do." Not only is it an excellent way to sharpen your own skills, it is very rewarding to have your student tell you that you made a positive difference in his real estate career. If you are interested in training, there is a national organization of real estate educators: The Real Estate Educators Association (REEA). Through their national and local organizations, they provide a professional affiliation for real estate educators. They award the DREI designation (Designated Real Estate Instructor) for excellence in training. For more information, write to REEA at One Illinois Center #200, 111 East Wacker Drive, Chicago, IL 60601. Check, too, local REEA chapters, which provide support groups for trainers.

Relocation Specialist

For those who prefer a salaried job, relocation may be the specialty to choose. To help people move across the nation, real estate companies and private relocation firms both provide referral services. Generally, a licensed real estate agent is the relocation counselor. A member of that particular relocation network provides a lead (name of a relocating buyer or seller) to the relocation counselor. Upon receiving a name, the counselor calls the party and conducts an interview to find out all about the transferee's needs. Then the relocation counselor contacts an real estate agent in the area where the transferee wants to relocate. The agent pays a referral fee to the relocation company from the commission paid when the agent sells a home to the transferee. Although the salary of a relocation counselor is generally no more than the REALTOR® national average, it *is* a salaried position. After agents find out how erratic commission sales can be, some rush for a salary!

Those are the most common growth and specialty areas that you may want to consider after your career is in full swing. In addition, some licensees become property managers, go into commercial real estate sales or become representatives for related services businesses such as title insurance and mortgage banking. Your experience as a successful salesperson is invaluable in any of these specialty areas. For, no matter what you do, or with whom you do it, we all really sell every day—sell a product, a service or ourselves.

A Look into a Crystal Ball

Throughout this book, I have shown you how real estate sales is evolving—and how you and your career are part of this evolution. As you move toward your decision to start your career, here are those trends—and some predictions further into the future. After all, you want to know the long-term potential for your career advancement.

The Rich Are Getting Richer

Owners and managers across the country report that the best agents are capturing more of the business, while the income of the low to midrange agents is sliding downward. Why? The business has become more technically complex. Costs of getting into and staying in the business have risen. The consumer is more demanding. To be successful, agents must invest in themselves continually. I see this division of agents as I teach real estate courses. In every class, there is one large group of experienced agents who resist investing in the materials, education and training that they must have to compete today. But, there is always a much smaller group who eagerly grasps these new concepts, spends the money and, of course, will capture the customer. According to the National Association of REALTORS®, there will be fewer licensees nationally as this decade continues. But, these licensees will be more dedicated, capable and successful. For those of you who want to make real estate a career and are willing to invest in yourself this is a wonderful era of opportunity.

Experience Will Count

With fewer agents in the business, the years of experience per agent will increase. This, in itself, is good for the industry. One of the heartbreaking facts of real estate sales is that few people go into the business understanding it; they leap before they look. Too many agents merely give it a try and get out of the business quickly. This turnover hurts the image of an agent and certainly hurts the consumer, who expects a high level of professional service. Few agents with more experience will ultimately enhance the image of our industry.

It Will Be Tougher To Get Hired as a New Agent

As managers discover the costs of indiscriminately hiring agents who fail, they will become much more selective in their hiring practices. And, managers will work more closely with their new agents to assure their success. This means to you that you will get a higher level of consulting service from your manager, so that you can get started—fast! It also means that, as an experienced agent, you will be working with carefully chosen people who will be a benefit to your business.

Only the Smartest Companies Are Staying in Business

Only the smartest companies will continue to stay in business. As profits have shrunk and costs have gone up, companies who haven't run "lean and mean" have gone out of business. The days of the mom-and-pop real estate office are gone. To get the business expertise they need to run a real estate company, many companies have affiliated locally or nationally. This trend will continue. I do not mean that small companies cannot survive in this decade. However, a small company must focus on a specific market and serve that market beautifully. Just as real estate agents are becoming specialists, so do these small companies survive and prosper by becoming specialists in new home sales, condominium sales, waterfront properties, farmland, etc.

Agents Must Manage Commissions Better To Profit

Companies are getting less of the total commission dollars. The National Association of REALTORS® predicts that this trend will continue. Agents will be paid a relatively higher percent of the gross commission, while the company is paid relatively less from each transaction. This sounds great to you, right? Maybe. What that means, though, is that the responsibility for allocating dollars and budgeting falls increasingly onto the agent's shoulders. This switch is most easily seen in advertising budgets. Fifteen years ago, the company collected enough money to allocate a generous amount to newspaper advertising. Today, this same company does not have those advertising dollars. So, they must carefully budget and allocate their newspaper advertising dollars to get the biggest "bang for the buck." Ten years ago, if you asked for another ad, your manager said "Sure." Today, your manager can't afford to say yes. Because agents get more commission dollars, they must spend some of their own dollars to advertise their listings. So, the agent becomes a minicompany, with the responsibility of planning, budgeting and allocating his or her own dollars to newspaper advertising—if the agent wants to advertise his or her listings.

Historically, the agent did not have to worry about planning, budgeting and measuring marketing results with his own money. Now, it is a real challenge for an agent to learn to be his or her own "owner." One of the poignant trends observed in experienced agents is resistance to these changes. Agents who have been in the business ten years or more still have a "50/50 mentality on a 70/30 split." They just cannot break loose from their own commission dollars, even though they know that the company cannot provide some of the services it provided ten years ago. That is why these agents are languishing, while agents who are good career planners are thriving. In the nineties, companies will provide guidance to agents to learn the same planning and budgeting process that companies have used to be profitable. I have created a "professional's business planning system" to help each agent become a profitable "owner" of his or her own business. I use it to counsel with each agent in my office, so they can be highly profitable. As your career develops, get the business planning expertise you need to ensure that you will not waste your marketing dollars—and that you will personally make a profit.

Technology Rules

When I began my real estate career, agents had no computers, no printers and no multiple listing books full of properties. Instead, every day, we got 20 to 50 new listings, printed on colored half-sheets of paper. Our job, should we choose to complete it, was to sort all those listings and put them in the right section of our personal file. A few people in our office were great collators. Their job description, as they saw it, was to organize their real estate information. Not I. My job was to sell real estate. But, I couldn't sell real estate unless I had knowledge of the properties available. So, I just asked the collators if I could use their files—and I sold houses! Sounds cruel, doesn't it, using someone else's files? But, they got recognition for organizing. They liked the idea that their files were used to sell houses. They just didn't want to be the people who sold the houses! They actually sold one to two homes a year. They liked coming to the office but just did not like dealing with buyers and sellers.

Today, it is even easier to get caught in the organization process. Now, all kinds of gizmos, gadgets and electronic tools can take up all of our time. However, used properly, these tools can organize and assist our business. As in the filing example, it is a matter of degree. Agents are using fax machines, computer software and telephone communication tools to streamline and enhance their businesses. Teaching a management class in Walnut Creek last year, I even saw a visual map display on a screen in an agent's car. The agent explained that the maps were created through his programming his in-car computer and used to find his way showing property! (Actually, I think it was used to impress the customer. That's okay—to some extent.)

Before you get sold on a piece of electronic wizardry, ask yourself, "What is this program for? Does it help me save time and get in front of more people? Is it to impress someone? Does it keep me away from the sales cycle? In the nineties, to compete, agents will have to invest in the tools that streamline their businesses.

Coming into the business now gives you an advantage. You can look at these tools with a fresh eye, and use your expertise from your former business, avocation or life experience to make smart buying decisions. Remember, there is a huge business today in real estate products. The people creating those products have a great market—all those real estate agents who come into the business each year. Get advice from your manager before you invest in anything.

Summary

If you have wanted to open your own business, with relatively low start-up costs and high income potential, a real estate career is a good choice. There has never been a better time for a dedicated careerist to go into the field. As you can see from the information just given you, the trends of the nineties all focus on the agent as careerist. This book was created to help people like you get all the information you need to make a smart business decision. We need people like you to create careerist success. Our consumers demand—and deserve—a high level of service. Through taking the careerist approach, you can give the consumer exactly what he or she wants. That will get you what you want—an exciting, challenging, creative, profitable career. Take advantage of the momentum of the nineties. Start your career now. The best of the business to you!

Appendix A:
Survey Results

Expectations of New Agents

Here are the results of a survey completed by 117 agents with less than three months in residential real estate sales. The survey was gathered during a postlicense practices of real estate course; the participants were surveyed between July 1992 and March 1993. This survey shows the expectations of these new agents, hired as full-timers. These expectations are compared to the median income figures for REALTORS®.

1. Your expected income for this year—figure one year from your practices course graduation:

8%	expected incomes from	$12,000 to $20,000
20%	expected incomes from	$21,000 to $30,000
35%	expected incomes from	$31,000 to $50,000
30%	expected incomes from	$51,000 to $75,000
11%	expected incomes over	$75,000

The median income for all REALTORS® (about half the licensees in the United States) is $22,500. This means that almost 92 percent of the new agents surveyed expected an income in their first year to exceed that of the median income—for all REALTORS®!

2. The number of sales and listings sold that this represents in your office:

    - Approximately one-third of those surveyed could translate their desired income into sales and listings sold.
    - Approximately one-third of those surveyed guessed at what their income expectations meant in terms of dollars.
    - Approximately one-third of those surveyed had no idea of what their income expectations meant in terms of numbers of homes sold.

This answer indicates that the new real estate agents surveyed are not getting the information they need to tie their income expectations to the amount of work they must complete to reach these income expectations (listings sold and sales).

Without this information, agents new to the business may conclude that it is easy to make lots of money in real estate sales—just sell a few homes a year.

3. When do you expect to receive your first check?

13%	Less than 30 days
49%	30–60 days
34%	61–90 days
4%	91–180 days
—	over 180 days

It takes approximately 45 to 60 days after a sale is written for an agent to receive a paycheck. Because 62 percent of the respondents expect to get a check within their first 60 days in the business, they intend to walk out of class and immediately sell a home! (Is it possible that they do not know the time frame involved in finding a qualified buyer?) A more realistic expectation for a paycheck is 90 to 120 days. These agents' unrealistic expectations may lead them to consider themselves failures when they do not immediately sell a home and get a quick paycheck.

4. How long can you go without income and remain in real estate?

7%	Less than 3 months
16%	3–4 months
30%	5–6 months
46%	over 6 months

Twenty-three percent of the respondents said they could go without income only four months or less and stay in real estate. According to a National Association of REALTORS® survey of home-buyers, purchasers look for a home an average of 16 weeks before making a buying decision. Because it takes approximately two months to close a home from the time the purchase agreement is written, new agents, on average, take four months to meet, show and sell a prospect. Then, a home takes two months to close. That is a total of six months. Of course, a new agent may quickly meet a purchaser ready to buy, and may be able to sell and close the home more quickly. But, the chance of finding, showing, selling and closing a home more quickly than three to four months is remote. Are new agents' savings resources adequate to allow them the time necessary to create a strong real estate career?

5. As a first-year agent, what is the minimum number of sales and listings sold that you must complete to be retained by your manager in your office?

Seventy-one percent of the respondents did not know their managers' minimum expectations of them. Without minimum, stated productivity standards set by management, new agents do not know what is expected of them. Clear expectations and a plan to get there assure that both the agent and the manager are on the same track, committed to reaching a common goal. Then, a business plan can be created, a plan that spells out the daily activities the new agent needs to complete to reach his or her stated goal—and the manager's minimum productivity standards.

Appendix B: Directory of Real Estate License Law Officials (by Jurisdiction)

Alabama

D. Phillip Lasater
Real Estate Commission
1201 Carmichael Way
Montgomery, AL 36106
205-242-5544

Alaska

Grayce A. Oakley
Division of Occupational
  Licensing
3601 C St., Suite 722
Anchorage, AK 99503
907-563-2169

Alberta

Rudolph J. Palovcik
Consumer and Corporate Affairs
19th Floor, 10025 Jasper Ave.
Edmonton, Alberta, Canada
  T5J 3Z5
403-422-1588

Arizona

Jerry A. Holt
Department of Real Estate
202 E. Earil Dr. #400
Phoenix, AZ 85012
602-279-2909

Arkansas

Roy L. Bilheimer
Real Estate Commission
612 South Summit St.
Little Rock, AR 72201-4740
501-682-2732

British Columbia

P. Dermot Murphy
Real Estate Council of British
   Columbia
Suite 900-750 West Pender St.
Vancouver, British Columbia,
   Canada V6C 2T8
604-683-9664

California

Clark Wallace
Department of Real Estate
185 Berry St., Rm. 3400
San Francisco, CA 94107
415-904-5900

Colorado

Michael B. Gorham
Department of Regulatory
   Agencies
Real Estate Commission
12776 Logan St.—4th Floor
Denver, CO 80203
303-894-2166

Connecticut

Laurence L. Hannafin
Department of Consumer
   Protection
Real Estate Division
165 Capitol Ave., Rm. G-8
Hartford, CT 06106
203-566-5130

Delaware

Dave Hill
Department of Administrative
   Services
O'Neill Building
P.O. Box 1401
Dover, DE 19902
302-739-4522

District of Columbia

Leon W. Lewis
Dept. of Consumer &
   Regulatory Affairs
614 H Street N.W., Rm. 913
P.O. Box 37200
Washington, DC 20013-7200
202-727-7853

Florida

Darlene F. Keller
Department of Professional
   Regulation
Division of Real Estate
400 W. Robinson St.
Orlando, FL 32801
407-423-6053

Georgia

Charles Clark
Real Estate Commission
Suite 500—Sussex Place
148 International Blvd., N.E.
Atlanta, GA 30303-1734
404-656-3916

Guam

Joaquin G. Blaz
Insurance, Securities, Banking
& Real Estate Division
855 West Marine Dr.
Agana, GU 96910
671-477-5145

Hawaii

Calvin T. Kimura
Real Estate Commission
Department of Commerce &
Consumer Affairs
250 S. King St., Rm. 702
Honolulu, HI 96813
808-586-2643

Idaho

Jeri Pyeatt
Real Estate Commission
Statehouse Mail
Boise, ID 83720-6000
208-334-3285

Illinois

Julie A. Mategrano
Department of Professional
Regulation
320 W. Washington St.
Springfield, IL 62786
217-782-7466

Indiana

Gerald Quigley
Professional Licensing Agency
1021 Government Center North
100 North Senate Ave.
Indianapolis, IN 46204
317-232-2980

Iowa

Roger L. Hansen
Professional Licensing &
Regulation Division
Real Estate Commission
1918 S.E. Hulsizer Avenue
Ankeny, IA 50021
515-281-3183

Kansas

E. W. Yockers
Real Estate Commission
Landon State Office Bldg.
900 Jackson St., Rm. 501
Topeka, KS 66612-1220
913-296-3411

Kentucky

W. Chris Alford
Real Estate Commission
10200 Linn Station Rd., Ste. 201
Louisville, KY 40223
502-425-4273

Louisiana

J. C. Willie
Real Estate Commission
P.O. Box 14785
Baton Rouge, LA 70898-4785
504-925-4771

Maine

Carol J. Leighton
Real Estate Commission
State House Station #35
Augusta, ME 04333
207-582-8727

Maryland

Elizabeth A. Beggs
Real Estate Commission
501 St. Paul Place, 8th Floor
Baltimore, MD 21202
410-333-6230

Massachusetts

Joseph R. Autilio
Board of Registration of Real
    Estate Brokers & Salesman
Real Estate Board
100 Cambridge St., Rm. 1518
Boston, MA 02202
617-727-2373

Michigan

Ann Millben
Department of Commerce
BOPR—Office of Commercial
    Services
Licensing Division
P.O. Box 30243
Lansing, MI 48909
517-373-0490

Minnesota

Barbara M. Lessard
Commerce Department
133 East 7th St.
St. Paul, MN 55101
612-296-2488

Mississippi

John W. Neelley
Real Estate Commission
1920 Dunbarton Dr.
Jackson, MS 39216-5087
601-987-3969

Missouri

Janet Brandt Thomas
Real Estate Commission
P.O. Box 1339
Jefferson City, MO 65102
314-751-2628

Montana

Grace A. Berger
Department of Commerce
Board of Realty Regulation
111 N. Jackson
Helena, MT 59620
406-444-2961

Nebraska

Les Tyrrell
Real Estate Commission
301 Centennial Mall South
P.O. Box 94667
Lincoln, NE 68509-4667
402-471-2004

Nevada

George W. Whitney
Real Estate Division
1665 Hot Springs Rd.
Capitol Complex
Carson City, NV 89710
702-687-4280

New Brunswick

Carl Sherwood
Real Estate Council
P.O. Box 785
Fredericton, New Brunswick,
    Canada E3B 5B4
506-455-9733

New Hampshire

John P. Cummings
Real Estate Commission
95 Pleasant St.
Spaulding Bldg.
State Office Park South
Concord, NH 03301
603-271-2701

New Jersey

Micki Greco Shillito
Real Estate Commission
20 West State St.
CN-328
Trenton, NJ 08625
609-292-8280

New Mexico

Jim Apodaca
Real Estate Commission
1650 University Blvd., N.E.
    Ste. 490
Albuquerque, NM 87102
505-841-9120

North Carolina

Phillip T. Fisher
Real Estate Commission
P.O. Box 17100
Raleigh, NC 27619-7100
919-733-9580

North Dakota

Dennis D. Schultz
Real Estate Commission
314 East Thayer Ave.
Bismarck, ND 58502
701-224-2749

Ohio

Dennis Tatum
Division of Real Estate
77 South High St.
Columbus, OH 43266-0547
614-466-4100

Oklahoma

Norris Price
Real Estate Commission
4040 N. Lincoln Blvd., Suite 100
Oklahoma City, OK 73105
405-521-3387

Ontario

Gordon J. Randall
Real Estate & Business Brokers
  Act
555 Yonge St., 3rd Floor
Toronto, Ontario, Canada
  M7A 2H6
416-326-8680

Oregon

Morella Larsen
Real Estate Agency
158—12th St. N.E.
Salem, OR 97310-0240
503-378-4170

Pennsylvania

Teresa A. Woodall
Real Estate Commission
Bureau of Professional &
  Occupational Affairs
Room 611, Transportation &
  Safety Bldg.
P.O. Box 2649
Harrisburg, PA 17105-2649
717-783-3658

Quebec

Real Martel
Service du Cortage Immobilier
  du Quebec
Ministere Des Finances
220, Grande-Allee Est,
  Suite 910
Quebec, Canada G1R 2J1
418-643-4597

Saskatchewan

Kirk Bacon
Real Estate Commission
#107—3929—8th Street East
Saskatoon, Saskatchewan,
  Canada S7H 5M2
307-374-5233

South Carolina

Henry L. Jolly
Real Estate Commission
1201 Main St., Suite 1500
Columbia, SC 29201
803-737-0700

South Dakota

Larry G. Lyngstad
Real Estate Commission
P.O. Box 490
Pierre, SD 57501-0490
605-773-3600

Tennessee

Bruce E. Lynn
Real Estate Commission
500 James Robertson Parkway
Suite 180, Volunteer Plaza
Nashville, TN 37243-1151
615-741-2273

Texas

Wallace Collins
Real Estate Commission
P.O. Box 12188
Austin, TX 78711-2188
512-459-6544

Utah

Blaine E. Twitchell
Department of Commerce
Division of Real Estate
P.O. Box 45806
Salt Lake City, UT 84145-0806
801-530-6747

Virgin Islands

Marylyn A. Stapleton
Depart. of Licensing &
  Consumer Affairs
Bldg. #1 Subbase
Property & Procurement Bldg.,
  Rm. 205
St. Thomas, VI 00802
809-774-3130

Virginia

Joan L. White
Department of Commerce
3600 West Broad St., 5th Floor
Richmond, VA 23230-4917
804-367-8552

Washington

Sydney W. Beckett
Department of Licensing
Professional Licensing Services
Real Estate Program
P.O. Box 9015
Olympia, WA 98507-9015
206-586-6101

West Virginia

Richard E. Strader
Real Estate Commission
1033 Quarrier Street, Suite 400
Charleston, WV 25301-2315
304-558-3555

Wisconsin

Cletus J. Hanson
Department of Regulation &
  Licensing
Bureau of Direct Licensing &
  Real Estate
1400 East Washington Ave.,
  Rm. 281
P.O. Box 8935
Madison, WI 53708
608-267-7134

Wyoming

Constance K. Anderson
Real Estate Commission
205 Barrett Bldg.
Cheyenne, WY 82002
307-777-7141

Appendix C: Resources for Success

The following books (except where noted), are published by the Real
Estate Education Company, a division of Dearborn Financial Publishing, Inc., 520 N. Dearborn Street, Chicago, IL 60610. 1-800-322-
8621.

Real Estate Principles for State Licensing Exam Study

Modern Real Estate Practice, 13th Edition, by Fillmore W. Galaty,
Wellington J. Allaway and Robert C. Kyle, 1993.

Study Guide for Modern Real Estate Practice, 13th Edition, by Edith
Lank, consulting editor, 1993. A supplement for prelicense courses.

Real Estate Fundamentals, 4th Edition, by Wade E. Gaddy, Jr., and
Robert E. Hart, 1993. Suited for streamlined or concentrated
courses.

The Language of Real Estate, 4th Edition, by John W. Reilly, 1993.
Handbook for mastering real estate terminology.

Questions and Answers To Help You Pass the Real Estate Exam, 4th Edition, by John W. Reilly and Paige Bovee Vitousek, 1992. Simulates the actual format of the state licensing exam.

Real Estate Exam Guide: Designed for ASI Sales and Broker Exams, 3rd Edition, by William H. Pivar, 1992. Review of concepts covered on the licensing exam prepared by ASI.

Guide to Passing the PSI Real Estate Exam, by Lawrence Sager, 1992. Overview of concepts tested on licensing exam prepared by PSI.

State-Specific Supplements

Real Estate Education Company offers many texts that address specific laws and practices in a particular state.

Law and Agency

Real Estate Law, 3rd Edition, by Frank Gibson, James Karp and Elliot Klayman, 1992.

Agency Relationships in Real Estate, by John W. Reilly, 1987.

Buyer Agency: Your Competitive Edge in Real Estate, 2nd Edition, by Gail Lyons and Don Harlan, 1993.

Real Estate Math

Mastering Real Estate Mathematics, 5th Edition, by William L. Ventolo, Jr., Wellington J. Allaway and G. E. Irby, 1989.

Real Estate Math: Explanations, Problems, Solutions, 4th Edition, by George Gaines, Jr., and David S. Coleman, 1990. Assumes little knowledge of math; format parallels school and state licensing exams.

Books on Sales Careers

Your Successful Real Estate Career, by Kenneth W. Edwards, American Management Association, 1993.

Effective Real Estate Sales and Marketing, 2nd Edition, by Johnnie Rosenauer, 1988.

Fast Start in Real Estate Sales, by Karl Breckenridge, 1989.

Power Real Estate Selling, 2nd Edition, by William H. Pivar, 1988.

Power Real Estate Listing, 2nd Edition, by William H. Pivar, 1988.

World Class Selling: How To Turn Adversity into Success, by Art Mortell, 1991.

List for Success: How Real Estate Professionals Make Big Money, by Jim Londay, 1986.

References

Horizons, A Look at the Twenty-First Century. A synopsis and analysis of the surveys completed by the National Association of REALTORS®, 777 14th Street N.W., Washington, DC 20005. 1-800-874-6500, published January 1992.

Real Estate Brokerage 1991: Income, Expenses, Profits. An analysis of residential REALTOR® firms that answered a survey from the National Association of REALTORS®. Compiled by the Research Division of the National Association of REALTORS®, 777 14th Street N.W., Washington, DC 20005. 1-800-874-6500.

The Homebuying and Selling Process 1991. An analysis of a survey sent to a sample of 20,000 homebuyers in December 1991. Compiled by the Research Division of the National Association of REALTORS®, 777 14th Street N.W., Washington, DC, 20005. 1-800-874-6500.

1993 Digest of Real Estate License Laws. A reference guide of license law statistics compiled by the National Association of Real Estate License Law Official (NARELLO) from materials gathered by NARELLO committees. P. O. Box 129, Centerville, UT 84014. 801-298-5572.

30 Days to Dollars. A start-up business plan for the new agent; assures income fast. Carla Cross Seminars, 1070 Idylwood Dr. S.W., Issaquah, WA 98027. 206-392-6914.

The Recruiter, a manager's personal recruiting presentation. Carla Cross Seminars, 1070 Idylwood Drive S.W., Issaquah, WA 98027. 206-392-6914.

Education

Graduate REALTORS® Institute (GRI), 100, 200, and 300 level series of courses, when completed, lead to the GRI designation. Purpose: To provide the basic information necessary to create a successful real estate career. Provided by State REALTOR® Associations. Call your local State Association for dates and locations.

Certified Residential Specialist (CRS), a series of seven courses, any three of which provide partial qualification to earn the CRS designation. For information on the courses and the designation, write to the Residential Sales Council, 430 N. Michigan Ave., Chicago, IL 60611. 1-800-462-8841.

Certified Real Estate Broker (CRB), a comprehensive series of one-day courses, focusing on the various aspects of real estate management; completing the courses, plus fulfilling other requirements leads to the CRB designation. For information, write to the Real Estate Brokerage Managers Council, 430 N. Michigan Ave., Chicago, IL 60611. 1-800-621-8738.

Certified Commercial Investment Member (CCIM), a series of 14 courses, created for the commercial specialist. The completion of a combination of these courses, plus meeting other requirements, leads to the CCIM designation. For information, write to the Commercial Investment Real Estate Institute, P. O. Box 109025, 430 N. Michigan Ave., Chicago, IL 60611. 1-800-621-7027.

Index